Improving social housing through transfer

LONDON: The Stationery Office

Ordered by the
House of Commons

This report has been prepared under Section 6 of the National Audit Act 1983 for presentation to the House of Commons in accordance with Section 9 of the Act.

John Bourn
Comptroller and Auditor General

National Audit Office
13 March 2003

The National Audit Office study team consisted of:

Paul Wright-Anderson, Keith Holden, Chris Dalgarno-Platt, Tracey Payne and Mandy Neer under the direction of Joe Cavanagh

This report can be found on the National Audit Office web site at www.nao.gov.uk

For further information about the National Audit Office please contact:

National Audit Office
Press Office
157-197 Buckingham Palace Road
Victoria
London
SW1W 9SP

Tel: 020 7798 7400

Email: enquiries@nao.gsi.gov.uk

Contents

Cover image courtesy of PRP Architects.

Summary

1 This Report focuses on two programmes for transferring social housing in England from local authorities to Registered Social Landlords (RSLs)[1]. These programmes aim to improve the condition of social housing and the quality of housing services provided to tenants. The Large Scale Voluntary Transfer (LSVT) programme started in 1988 and is still running, while transfers under the Estates Renewal Challenge Fund (ERCF) programme ran from September 1996 to March 2000. Responsibility for both programmes rests with the Office of the Deputy Prime Minister (the Office).

2 Transfer entails an RSL using private finance to buy and renovate all or some of a local authority's homes. ERCF transfers entailed the Office paying RSLs grants to compensate them for taking over homes that had negative values. By February 2003, 143 local authorities had carried out 180 transfers of a total of 738,000 homes, representing 18 per cent of the 4.2 million homes owned by local authorities at the start of the LSVT programme in 1988.

3 Our report complements the Audit Commission's report[2] on how transferring local authorities have carried out their continuing responsibilities for housing. Together, our reports provide a comprehensive assessment of the success of the LSVT and ERCF transfer programmes.

4 Successive governments have supported the policy of housing transfer[3] and the programme has been a significant plank of housing policy since its introduction in 1988, on the grounds that:

- transfer could provide an important vehicle to bring forward the improvement of sub-standard local authority housing at a time when public funding could not be made available;
- transfer was part of a wider government agenda of accessing private finance to support public services;

---

1 *Registered Social Landlords (RSLs) are independent housing organisations registered with the Housing Corporation under the Housing Act 1996. Most RSLs are housing associations but RSLs also include trusts, co-operatives and companies.*

2 *Housing After Transfer (2002) - a summary of the key conclusions is at Appendix 4.*

3 *For example, most recently in the Housing Policy Statement 2000 "Quality and Choice: The way forward for housing" (paragraphs 4.13 to 4.20).*

- transfer could bring additional benefits of greater tenant choice and participation, and of risk transfer, and therefore had the potential to be a better alternative to local authority retention even if the local authority had funds available; and
- the separation of landlord and strategic housing functions could be beneficial, and in some local authorities retention might not be desirable or feasible because of weaknesses in the management and oversight of authorities' housing departments.

Our report looks at whether transfers have delivered the intended benefits for tenants, and at the financial effects of transfer. We have not looked at the policy question of whether public funding could have been made available, or at the quality of local authorities' housing management as we are not the auditors of local authorities.

Main Findings

5 Our principal findings are:

On delivering improved services to tenants

i A key objective of the programme has been to bring in private finance to secure improvements in the quality of housing, especially by renovating stock in poor condition, and better services to tenants. Since 1988, RSLs have raised £11.6 billion of private finance, of which £5.4 billion has been used to purchase the stock. The remaining £6.2 billion represents finance which RSLs can draw on to meet future costs such as renovations as their long term improvement programmes proceed, transfer RSLs being required currently to secure 30 year funding at the time of transfer. Private finance secured through transfer was in part intended to help remedy some of the backlog of disrepair in local authority housing. The Office's English House Condition Survey of 1996 valued this backlog at £19 billion. How much of this backlog may have been tackled through transfer is not known currently. The Office's English House Condition Survey of 2001, expected to be published later this year will, however, provide an opportunity to measure the impact of transfer on the backlog of disrepair.

ii Transfers were also intended to break up local authorities' monopoly of social housing by giving tenants a choice of landlord. Transfers have reduced the proportion of social housing owned by local authorities in England from 90 per cent in 1988 to 70 per cent by 2001. In around two thirds of transfers, local authorities have sold their homes to new organisations created from the authorities' housing departments specifically to receive the stock. More generally whole stock transfers have been the primary transfer vehicle and hence the new organisations have displaced the local authority landlord as the principal supplier but without necessarily expanding choice for tenants. From the 2001 programme onwards, the Office has formally required authorities to involve tenants in the selection of a new landlord. Where a choice of new landlord is available, and could provide for an element of competition in the transfer, a key difficulty is winning the trust of tenants in respect of the different landlords to maintain tenants' overall support for transfer.

iii RSLs have largely delivered the expected benefits to tenants of better quality social housing, better housing services and opportunities for tenant participation. Our survey of RSLs, supported by audit visits, found that around 72 per cent of RSLs' homes have been improved, that almost all repairs had been made on time, and promises met on housing services. Most RSLs had kept rent increases within Housing Corporation guideline figures, and had met their promises on tenant participation. Our discussions with tenants also suggested that many considered that they had benefited from transfer. Fifteen per cent of the RSLs we surveyed said that they had not met or were delayed in meeting promises to develop new homes. Reasons included financial or regulatory problems, planning delays or insufficient grant funding from local authorities. Additionally, in some instances the promises were no longer considered appropriate because costs had increased significantly or local circumstances suggested that less social housing was needed.

iv In 2001 the Office introduced a new Public Services Agreement target to make all social housing decent by 2010, and the transfer programme is contributing towards achievement of this target. The Office undertook a survey in November 2001 of 105 transfer RSLs to assess RSLs' progress with their improvement programmes. Prior to 2001 these programmes would not have been planned in relation to the Decent Home standard. About 30 per cent of the 82 RSLs responding were likely to meet the standard within five years of transfer, and most should do so within ten years. Up to 17 per cent of transferred homes might not meet the Decent Home standard within 10 years though. Transfer RSLs are more optimistic, anticipating on average that it takes around seven years to eradicate non-decent stock. The Office and the Housing Corporation are working with local authorities and RSLs to ensure that they have suitable plans for meeting the Decent Home target over time. The standard is included in the Transfer guidelines, is reported on by RSLs, and will be included in the Office's planned monitoring and evaluation of the transfer programme.

v Local authorities and RSLs make promises about the benefits that transfers will bring to tenants. The extent and cost of these promises vary, principally because of the extensive renovation often needed to bring homes to an acceptable standard. However, promises are sometimes unclear, leaving tenants uncertain about what they can expect from transfers and hindering subsequent evaluation of RSLs' performance. While accepting the merit of clearly defined promises where possible and appropriate, the Office considers that there are situations where it is possible that the new landlord, local authority and tenants will not wish to be tied down to firm commitments or will be unable to make such commitments.

vi In our view, evaluation by the Office of the delivery of the intended benefits by individual transfers and the programme as a whole could have been more extensive as the programme developed, by greater monitoring of the outcomes achieved in individual transfers over time. In 2001, the Office commissioned consultants to develop a new monitoring system for the impact of individual transfers and an evaluation framework for assessing the overall impact of the Large Scale Voluntary Transfer programme. It expects these systems to be operational by Spring 2003 and to apply to all transfers from 2001 onwards.

vii Most RSLs have established sound finances after transfer. A small proportion have, however, experienced financial difficulties and a very few RSLs have had to merge with other more viable RSLs to overcome significant financial problems.

On the financial effects of transfer

viii The terms on which a transfer is made to an RSL are intended to be cost neutral (i.e. to generate neither a surplus nor a loss) for the RSL but this may not be achievable in practice. The Office and local authorities use a model agreed with HM Treasury to inform negotiations over the transfer value. This value, known as Tenanted Market Value, is usually less than the open market value reflecting, appropriately, the intended continued use of the properties for social housing rather than the most profitable alternative use. The Tenanted Market Value is calculated as the net present value of the RSLs' projected stream of income from renting out the transfer stock, less its expenditure stream. We found, however, that the model uses a fixed time period of 30 years whereas property lives vary, and the discount rate used in the model has been higher than RSLs' cost of capital.

ix In our view, the fixed parameters within the transfer valuation model mean that cost neutrality is unlikely to be achieved in practice, and may increase the taxpayers' contribution beyond that intended to reflect the cost of bringing properties up to an appropriate standard. Property lives and the discount rate can have a significant impact on the potential transfer value. Using data for our eight LSVT case studies, for example, we estimated that if the life of properties had been assessed as 40 years the potential transfer value would have increased by £51 million (14 per cent) compared with the actual transfer price of £356 million. The case study RSLs all considered that their transferred stock would have a value 30 years after transfer, in part because of the better repairs and maintenance associated with transfers. They also expected higher surpluses after 30 years, even after allowing for the costs of renewal programmes. Similarly, we calculated the potential transfer value of one of our case study transfers would have been £27.5 million (53 per cent) higher using the real cost of capital compared to the actual transfer price of £51.9 million. Whilst we acknowledge the Office's view that there is no evidence that higher prices would have been achievable had they been sought in these transfers, these illustrative calculations demonstrate that cost neutrality may not be achievable in practice, particularly where key parameters are fixed and are not adapted to take account of the circumstances of each potential transfer.

x In the cases we examined, we found that post transfer events had an impact on the cost neutral position intended at transfer. Some changes reflected the difference between actual performance and that forecast at the time of transfer, and reflected the risk transfer inherent in the programme. For example, renovations cost more or less than planned, demand was lower or higher than expected, or rent regimes changed. But other impacts reflected events such as the refinancing of loans by RSLs after transfer, the sale of property under the Right To Buy scheme, or the sale or redevelopment of land after transfer. We found that the possibility of these more foreseeable events occurring was not always recognised in the transfer terms.

xi RSLs are independent, not-for-profit organisations set up to meet the needs of their tenants and the local communities which they serve. RSLs do not distribute any dividends. When a new RSL registers with the Housing Corporation, the Corporation requires that its principal object must be to provide social rental housing, which must account for at least 50 per cent of the RSL's activity. Up to 49 per cent of an RSL's activities may be in non-social housing areas. In the cases we examined these uses included student accommodation, key worker homes or assisting other housing needs, or they may be market renting or wider regeneration projects. Cost neutrality in the transfer value is difficult to achieve in practice, as noted above, and in our view the Office and Corporation should look to increase their influence over how any surpluses are used, however, to encourage their application to further social housing objectives or those designed to develop sustainable communities.

xii The Office calculated the Public Sector Borrowing Requirement impacts of individual transfers and the programme as a whole, but not the actual cost to the taxpayer of the transfer of the 738,000 homes covered by LSVT and ERCF transfers up to February 2003[4]. However, at various times the Office has estimated the cost of future transfers. For example, in 2001 the Office estimated that continuation of the LSVT programme would cost the taxpayer £4,200 a home, spread over 30 years, which is £1,300 a home more than the equivalent renovation under local authority ownership if that were feasible. In terms of the potential total costs, in 2001 the Office estimated that the transfer of a million homes over 5 years would cost the taxpayer £4.2 billion spread over 30 years. The Office considers that the additional financial cost of transfer over local authority renovation has delivered non quantifiable benefits such as earlier improvement of poor condition social housing, community regeneration and increased tenant participation, and achieved risk transfer, including risks relating to income and cost, maintenance and risks arising from shortfalls in demand. It also considers the additional financial cost to be small in the context of over £15 billion allocated to housing expenditure in the same 5-year period 2001-02 to 2005-06. As our report shows, the programme has been largely successful in delivering improvements in services to tenants and in transferring the financial risks in holding properties for letting.

xiii HM Treasury has recently revised its guidance on financial appraisals, including the recommended discount rate which is now 3.5 per cent. The Office is currently considering the impact of these changes on its appraisal of the transfer programme, including any adjustments which might be necessary in valuing costs and benefits to take account of optimism bias[5] and risk transfer as set out in the Treasury guidance. The lower discount rate will increase further the difference between the financial costs of transfer to an RSL and those of local authority retention and renovation, but this increase may be offset by adjustments necessary to reflect optimism bias and risk transfer.

4 *For an explanation of the difference between PSBR effect and the real cost to the taxpayer, see paragraph 3.31 and Appendix 1.*

5 *Optimism bias represents the tendency for over-optimism in the appraisal of the outcome of projects.*

Recommendations

6 The Office's role is to assess applications from local authorities for a place on the transfer programme, examine the calculation of the transfer price and review consultation documents before they are sent to tenants. The Office also makes recommendations to the Secretary of State as to whether consent for transfer should be given. The Housing Corporation reviews prospective transfer RSLs' business plans, governance, management and staffing arrangements, and if satisfied registers the RSL. The Corporation is also responsible for the ongoing regulation of transfer RSLs' financial and operational performance.

7 On the basis of our report, we make the following recommendations. The Office should:

i Unless there are clear reasons why such definition is undesirable, require that all promises to tenants are clearly defined, measurable and time-related, including an explicit promise to meet the Decent Homes standard in a reasonable timescale. Where promises need to be changed, tenants' organisations or those tenants directly affected should be consulted and the Office or the Corporation should monitor changes to ensure taxpayers and tenants continue to receive at least the value for money intended originally.

ii Examine local authorities' option appraisals and satisfy itself that the authorities have assessed properly all options for improving their housing and services to tenants. The Office should provide guidance on how a new model should be used by local authorities and central government to assess value for money. The National Audit Office would be content to review and comment on any model as it is developed.

iii Continue its efforts to extend the range of choice of landlord, to achieve the best transfer terms for tenants at a reasonable price. The Office should explore further how greater choice and competition can be brought to bear without undermining tenant support where transfer offers the best option. Where a transfer has gone ahead successfully with choice or competition, the Office should identify and disseminate good practice, particularly on how to handle tenants' concerns. Consideration should be given to the possibility of

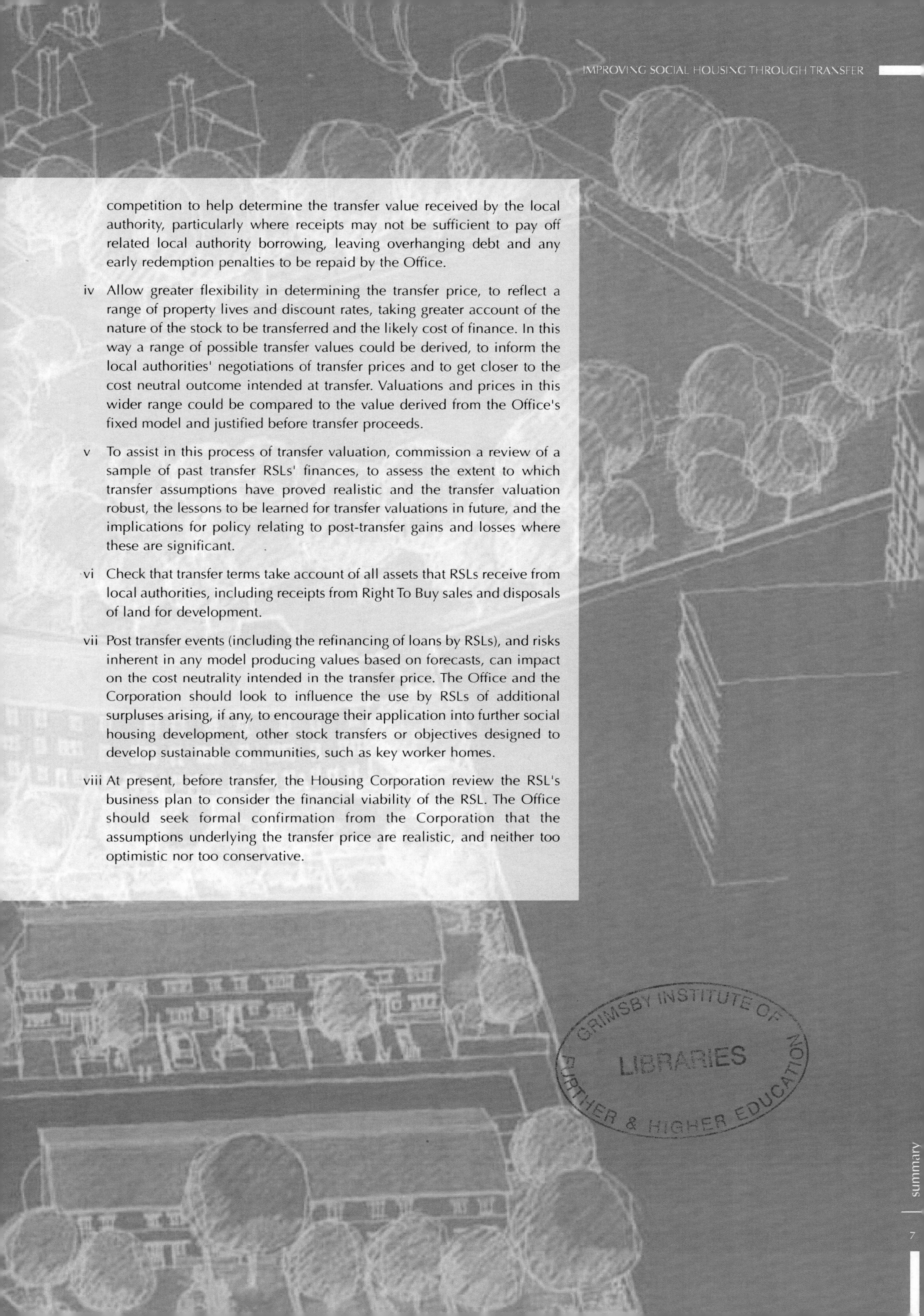

competition to help determine the transfer value received by the local authority, particularly where receipts may not be sufficient to pay off related local authority borrowing, leaving overhanging debt and any early redemption penalties to be repaid by the Office.

iv Allow greater flexibility in determining the transfer price, to reflect a range of property lives and discount rates, taking greater account of the nature of the stock to be transferred and the likely cost of finance. In this way a range of possible transfer values could be derived, to inform the local authorities' negotiations of transfer prices and to get closer to the cost neutral outcome intended at transfer. Valuations and prices in this wider range could be compared to the value derived from the Office's fixed model and justified before transfer proceeds.

v To assist in this process of transfer valuation, commission a review of a sample of past transfer RSLs' finances, to assess the extent to which transfer assumptions have proved realistic and the transfer valuation robust, the lessons to be learned for transfer valuations in future, and the implications for policy relating to post-transfer gains and losses where these are significant.

vi Check that transfer terms take account of all assets that RSLs receive from local authorities, including receipts from Right To Buy sales and disposals of land for development.

vii Post transfer events (including the refinancing of loans by RSLs), and risks inherent in any model producing values based on forecasts, can impact on the cost neutrality intended in the transfer price. The Office and the Corporation should look to influence the use by RSLs of additional surpluses arising, if any, to encourage their application into further social housing development, other stock transfers or objectives designed to develop sustainable communities, such as key worker homes.

viii At present, before transfer, the Housing Corporation review the RSL's business plan to consider the financial viability of the RSL. The Office should seek formal confirmation from the Corporation that the assumptions underlying the transfer price are realistic, and neither too optimistic nor too conservative.

Part 1

Introduction

Background

1.1 This Report focuses on two programmes for transferring social housing[6] in England from local authorities to Registered Social Landlords (RSLs). These programmes aim to improve the condition of social housing and the quality of housing services provided to tenants. The Large Scale Voluntary Transfer (LSVT) programme, the larger of the two programmes, started in 1988 and is still running, while transfers under the Estates Renewal Challenge Fund (ERCF) programme ran from September 1996 to March 2000. Both programmes were set up by the then-Department of the Environment, and responsibility now rests with the Office of the Deputy Prime Minister (the Office).

1.2 Transfer entails an RSL using private finance to buy a local authority's homes, with the authority then using the capital receipt to pay off any housing debts and any levy due to the Office. The authority may then use any monies left over for any purposes it sees fit. Where the transfer receipt is less than an authority's housing debts, the Office pays off such "overhanging debt" and any early redemption penalties. ERCF transfers entailed the Office paying grants to RSLs mainly as dowries, to compensate them for taking over homes that were typically on run-down, urban estates and that had negative values. Grants totalled £523 million.

1.3 The number of homes transferred has grown considerably since the programmes began, with the most rapid growth occurring in recent years (**Figure 1 overleaf**). By February 2003, 738,000 homes had been transferred - over 90 per cent under the LSVT programme - representing 18 per cent of the 4.2 million homes owned by local authorities at the start of the LSVT programme in 1988. There have been 180 transfers to RSLs across 143 local authorities[7], some authorities carrying out more than one transfer by selling off their stock in parts.

1.4 Although transfers have taken place across England, most early transfers were in the southern half of the country (**Figure 2 on page 11**) and fewer transfers have been in urban areas. However, the Office expects that an increasing proportion of the housing transferred in future will be relatively poor condition homes in urban areas. Transfers have provided the opportunity for tenants to vote on whether to have the local authority or an RSL as their landlord. Tenants have chosen to transfer rather than remain with their local authority in all but 46 of the proposed transfers. The largest transfer to date was Sunderland City Council's transfer of 36,356 homes in 2001. An even larger transfer, of 84,000 homes in Birmingham, was proposed but failed at a ballot in April 2002.

Why housing is transferred

1.5 Local authorities initiated the first transfers to take advantage of new powers provided under the Housing Acts 1985 and 1988, which allowed them to dispose of their housing and use the capital receipts for a variety of purposes, including funding the development of new housing and other capital works projects. Since April 2000, the Office has regarded transfer as making a major contribution towards achieving the Decent Homes standard[8] in all social housing by 2010 by bringing in private investment to help tackle the £19 billion backlog of disrepair in local authority housing that had been identified by the Office's English House Condition Survey of 1996. The rationale for transfers and how they should provide value for money are set out in **Figure 3 on page 12**.

6 *Social housing is affordable housing provided by local authorities and Registered Social Landlords for people who do not aspire, or cannot afford, to own or rent a home in the private sector.*

7 *On its Internet website, the Office maintains a list of all transfers of more than 500 homes at www.housing.odpm.gov.uk/transfers/download/lsvts.xls and a list of all ERCF transfers at www.housing.odpm.gov.uk/transfers/ercf/table.htm.*

8 *A Decent Home satisfies the following criteria: meets the minimum standards of the Housing Act 1985, is in a reasonable state of repair, has reasonably modern facilities, and provides a reasonable level of warmth.*

1 Homes transferred each year under the LSVT and ERCF programmes, 1988-89 to 2001-02

The number of homes transferred has grown considerably since the transfer programmes began, with the most rapid growth occurring in recent years.

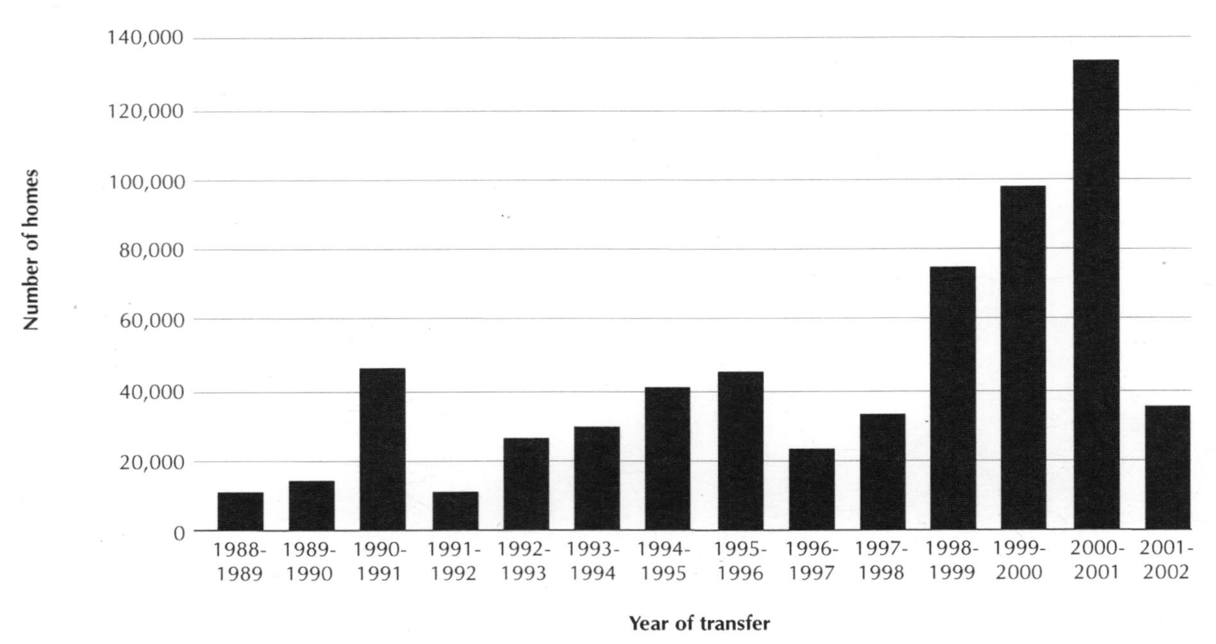

NOTE

Until 2000-01, local authorities that had been accepted on to the annual transfer programme had to complete their transfers within that year. Since then, the Office has allowed authorities two years to prepare for transfer. This change contributed to the fall in the number of homes transferred in 2001-02 compared with 2000-01. The Office expects 167,000 homes to be transfered in 2002-03.

Source: National Audit Office using data from the Office of the Deputy Prime Minister

Which organisations are involved and what they do in the transfer process

1.6 Local authorities, RSLs, the Office and the Housing Corporation are the principal bodies involved in transfers. It is for a local authority to decide on whether to embark on a transfer of its homes, having taken account of tenants' views and other options available to it, and to apply to the Office for a place on the annual transfer programme. The Office assesses the application and, if accepted, the local authority is then responsible for developing the details of its transfer scheme, consulting and balloting tenants, and negotiating a transfer price at which an RSL would take over the authority's stock. RSLs raise private finance to buy local authority stock and renovate it.

1.7 The Office becomes increasingly involved as the scheme proceeds. It examines in detail the calculation of the transfer price, including the costs of planned works, in consultation with the local authority and checks consultation documents before they are sent to tenants to ensure that consultation is sufficient and accurate. To help local authorities develop their transfer schemes, the Office has, since April 2001, provided advice and assistance through a Community Housing Task Force (the Task Force).

1.8 The Housing Corporation scrutinises the prospective RSL's business plan and governance, management and staffing arrangements to ensure that the landlord is financially sustainable and that the RSL will be well run. If satisfied, the Corporation registers the RSL, which is then subject to the Corporation's ongoing regulation of its financial and operational performance. In April 2000, in response to the growth and demands of the LSVT programme, the Corporation established a Stock Transfer Registration Unit as a specialist team to assess transfers.

2 Location of LSVT and ERCF stock transfers in English local authorities (by September 2002)

Local authorities across the whole country have transferred all or part of their housing stock

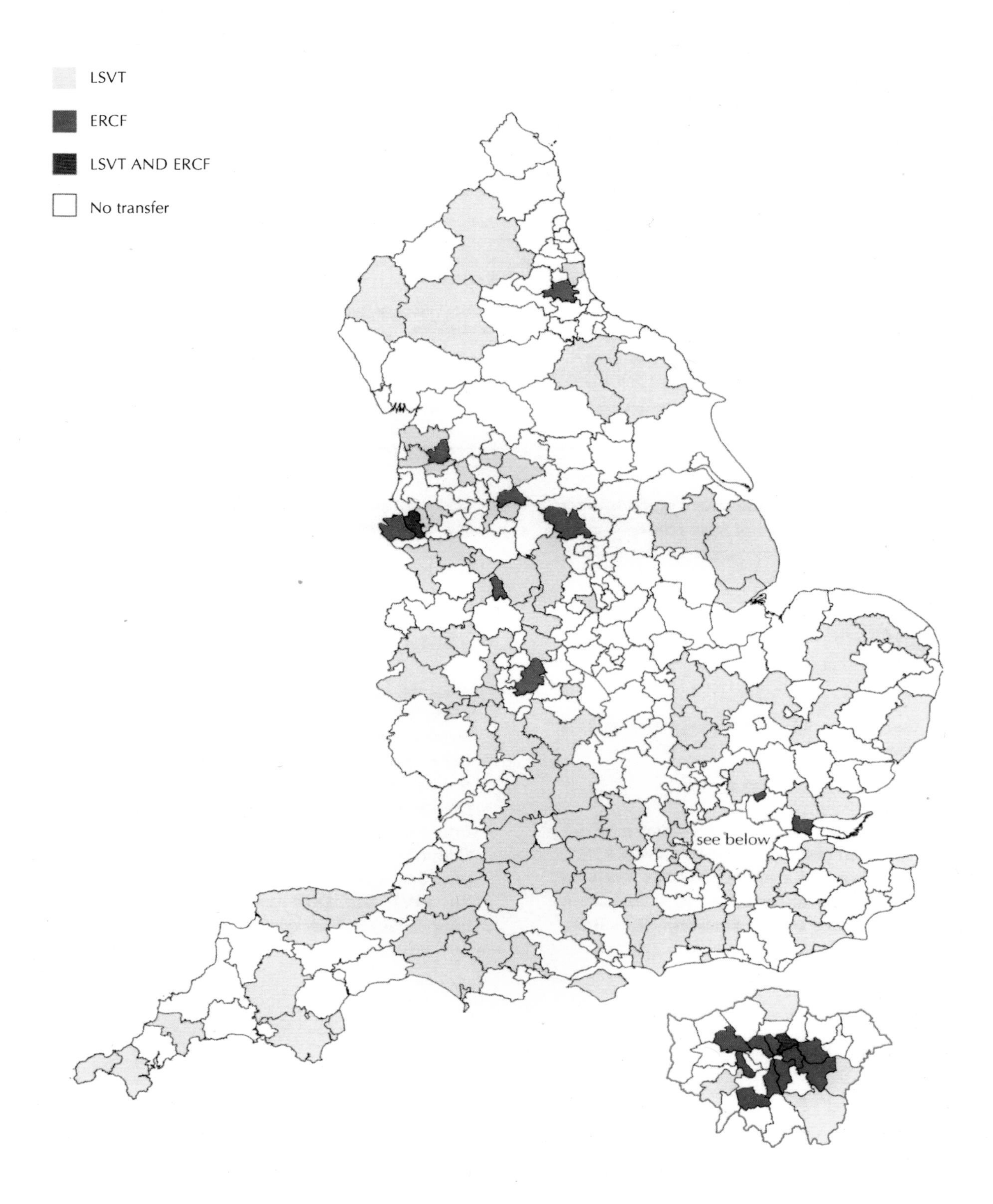

Source: Office of the Deputy Prime Minister

3 How transfers are intended to provide value for money

The Office expects transfers to be the best way of providing tenants with improved homes and housing services for the additional cost that falls to tenants and the taxpayer.

Major improvement programmes	1	At least for the first 10 years of the programme, RSLs were the only bodies able to raise private finance to fund major repairs programmes. More options have been available since 1998.
Better services	2	RSLs should provide a better quality of service, at a lower cost, than the local authority - through faster repairs and other services, and better management.
	3	RSLs should also provide more opportunity for tenant participation and choice of landlord.
	4	Local authorities should be better able to focus on their strategic role as a housing authority, if relieved of operational management of the service.
Sharing the costs	5	Major repairs programmes have a cost. This cost has in the past been borne by tenants (through higher rents). Part of the higher rent paid by tenants is passed on to taxpayers through Housing Benefit savings. Where the cost of renovation is not met by higher rents, the cost is borne by the taxpayer through lower transfer prices.
	6	Each transfer also involves the transaction costs of setting up the new body and arranging finance. This cost is usually borne by the taxpayer.
Transfers are value for money:	7	If the higher costs to tenants and taxpayers are outweighed by the benefits of improved homes and the better services referred to in 1 to 4 above, and
	8	If transfer provides the best way to achieve these benefits, compared to alternatives.

Source: National Audit Office

1.9 The Office then makes a final assessment of the transfer before recommending Secretary of State consent for the transfer to take place. The key stages in the transfer process are set out in **Figure 4**.

What we did

1.10 We examined:

- whether transfer has delivered the expected benefits (Part 2 of our report); and
- the financial effects of transfer (Part 3).

1.11 We used a variety of methods to obtain evidence for our report. These included case studies of 10 transfer RSLs[9], and a survey of these and a further 50 RSLs receiving transferred stock. We examined files and evaluation reports held by the Office and the Housing Corporation, and also analysed RSL performance data collected by the Corporation as part of its regulation of the RSL sector. We interviewed tenants and a range of stakeholders, and received advice and guidance from an expert panel. Our methods are set out in detail at Appendix 2 and further details of the 10 case study transfers are at Appendix 3.

1.12 Over the same time period as the National Audit Office study, the Audit Commission has been looking at how local authorities, which have transferred some or all of their housing stock, carry out their continuing responsibilities. We have worked closely with the Audit Commission, co-ordinating our fieldwork and sharing information. This report complements the Audit Commission's report, *Housing After Transfer*, together providing a comprehensive assessment of the success of the LSVT and ERCF transfer programmes from the perspectives of both central and local government.

9 *Broomleigh Housing Association, Broadacres Housing Association (formerly Hambleton Housing Association), Thanet Community Housing Association, Oakfern Housing Association (formerly Basingstoke & North Hampshire Housing Association), Manchester & District Housing Association, Spelthorne Housing Association, Ten Sixty-Six Housing Association, Poplar Housing and Regeneration Community Association, Fortunegate Community Housing and, Magna West Somerset Housing Association (Appendix 3 provides further details).*

4 Six key stages in the transfer process

Once a local authority has chosen to transfer its houses, it works closely with the Office, the RSL, the Housing Corporation and tenants to develop an acceptable scheme, culminating in the Secretary of State's consent for the transfer.

1 Local authority selects transfer as part of its housing strategy

Local authority (in consultation with tenants):

- considers options for housing (including transfer)
- consults the Office's Community Housing Task Force
- starts to develop transfer scheme
- selects prospective landlord

2 Local authority applies to the Office for place on transfer programme

The Office:

- assesses application against national criteria
- discusses valuation of homes and transfer price
- comments on development of transfer scheme

3 Local authority formally consults and ballots tenants

Local authority and prospective RSL:

- further develop transfer scheme
- discuss valuation and transfer price with the Office
- ballot tenants
- prepare for RSL registration with Housing Corporation
- prepare legal and financial agreements

4 Housing Corporation registers landlord

The Housing Corporation considers RSL's:

- independence from local authority
- governance
- staffing and management systems
- financial viability

5 The Secretary of State consents to the transfer

The Office advises on consent for transfer if:

- there has been adequate consultation with tenants
- the majority of tenants are not opposed to the transfer
- terms of transfer are acceptable
- public expenditure costs are value for money

6 Transfer takes place

After transfer, the Housing Corporation monitors RSL's:

- management and financial strength
- standards of probity and use of public resources

Source: National Audit Office

Part 2

The benefits of transfer

Transfers have attracted considerable sums of private finance for the repair and improvement of homes

2.1 Since 1988, RSLs have raised £11.6 billion (£12.8 billion at 2003 prices) of private finance to purchase local authority stock and pay for renovation of homes. RSLs have spent £5.4 billion (£6.0 billion at 2003 prices) purchasing the stock. The remaining £6.2 billion (£6.8 billion at 2003 prices) represents finance that RSLs may draw on to meet future costs such as renovations as their long term improvement programmes proceed, transfer RSLs being required currently to secure 30 year funding at the time of transfer. **Figure 5** shows the build up of private finance facilities since 1988. As the LSVT and ERCF transfer programmes have progressed, there has been an increase in the proportion of finance for renovating stock. This reflects the poorer quality stock, requiring more renovation, which has transferred in recent years.

2.2 Private finance secured through transfer was partly intended to address the backlog of disrepair in local authority housing. The Office's English House Condition Survey of 1996 valued this backlog at £19 billion. How much of this backlog has now been addressed through transfer is not known currently. The Office's English House Condition Survey of 2001, expected to be published later this year will, however, provide an opportunity to measure the impact of transfer on the backlog of disrepair. In future the Office will update the Survey annually.

5 Private finance raised by RSLs in receipt of transferred stock, 1988 to 2002

The amount of private finance available to transfer RSLs has steadily built up since transfers began in 1988, to be used to purchase stock and for future costs including those for renovation.

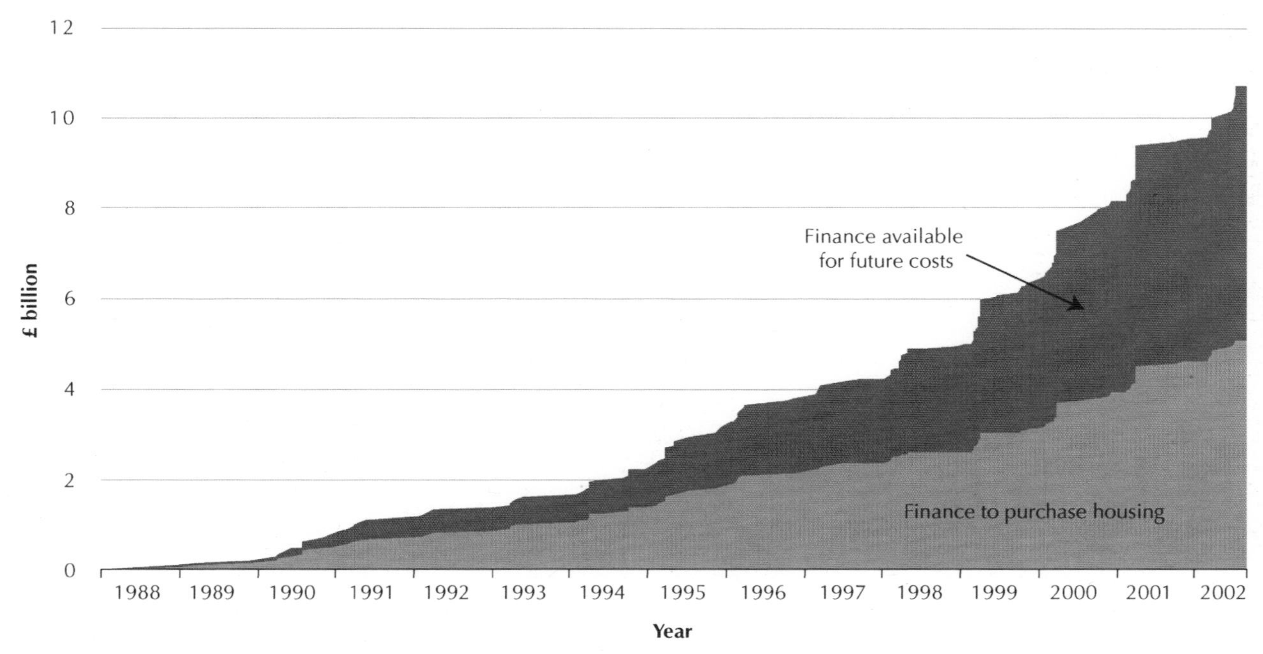

Source: National Audit Office, using information from the Office of the Deputy Prime Minister

Transfers have not significantly reduced the monopoly supply of social housing at the local level

2.3 Transfers have brought about a substantial shift in the social housing sector, as over 700,000 homes have been transferred from local authorities to RSLs. When transfers began in 1988, local authorities owned 90 per cent of the social housing in England **(Figure 6).** By 2001, their share had fallen to 70 per cent.

2.4 The Office intended that the transfer programmes would break up the monopoly supply of social housing. It set guidelines for the number of dwellings which could be transferred to a single landlord and precluded transfer RSLs from merging with neighbouring transfer RSLs. Transfers have exceeded the guideline maximum size in eight cases with the Office's approval because, for example, there were strong organisational reasons for not dividing up the stock or there were to be significant levels of demolition in areas of low demand. Some local authorities have split transferred stock between two or more RSLs within the same group structure to keep within the guideline size for a single RSL.

2.5 Between 1988 and July 2002, 103 transfers (61 per cent) involved a local authority transferring all its housing to one RSL (or one group). In around two thirds of transfers, local authorities have sold their homes to new organisations created from local authorities' housing departments and created specifically to receive the stock. More generally, whole stock transfers have been the primary transfer vehicle, and hence the transfer RSL has displaced the local authority landlord as the principal supplier but without necessarily expanding choice for tenants. Research undertaken by DTZ Pieda on behalf of the Office showed that 85 per cent of tenants in the six transfer RSLs covered in the research were satisfied with their landlord. The level of satisfaction with the landlord was the same before and after transfer but a higher proportion of local authority tenants (13 per cent) were "dissatisfied" compared to transfer tenants (7 per cent).

6 The shift in the ownership of social housing, 1988 to 2001

The number of homes owned by local authorities has fallen between 1988 and 2001 while the RSL sector has increased the size of its housing stock.

	Local authority homes	RSL homes	Total
1988	4.2 million	0.5 million	4.7 million
2001	2.9 million	1.3 million	4.2 million

NOTE

The fall by 0.5 million in the number of homes in the social housing sector is mainly due to the number of homes in both sectors sold under the Right To Buy scheme exceeding the number of new homes acquired or developed for social renting. A relatively small number of homes have been demolished during the period.

Source: Office of the Deputy Prime Minister

The promises and expected benefits of transfers made by local authorities and RSLs vary and are not always clear or measurable

2.6 After a local authority has decided to transfer its housing, it prepares a consultation document with the RSL setting out the benefits which the local authority and the RSL promise to deliver to tenants. The authority sends copies of the document to tenants, issues newsletters and holds public meetings to explain the expected benefits to tenants. The local authority then arranges for a secret ballot of tenants, giving all tenants an opportunity to vote for or against the proposed transfer.

2.7 The Office expects local authorities to follow a code of practice on publicity to ensure that consultation documents are objective about what tenants can expect from transfers. It encourages authorities to appoint an Independent Tenant Adviser to provide impartial advice to all tenants on the range of issues associated with a prospective transfer. Since 2001, the Office's Community Housing Task Force has also advised local authorities on their consultation of tenants. And the Office's transfer guidance has, since September 2001, set out good practice on local authority consultation with tenants.

2.8 Local authorities are required to submit their tenant consultation material to the Office and the Corporation for checking before the authorities send it to tenants. The Office and the Corporation aim to identify anything unacceptable to the Secretary of State which could affect the granting of consent to transfer, and to ensure that promises made are consistent with the RSLs' business plans.

2.9 Our survey of RSLs found that they and their local authorities had made a wide range of promises **(Figure 7).**

7 Areas in which benefits have been promised to tenants

Promises were most common in areas concerned with rents, home improvements and other works. They were least common in the area of local regeneration.

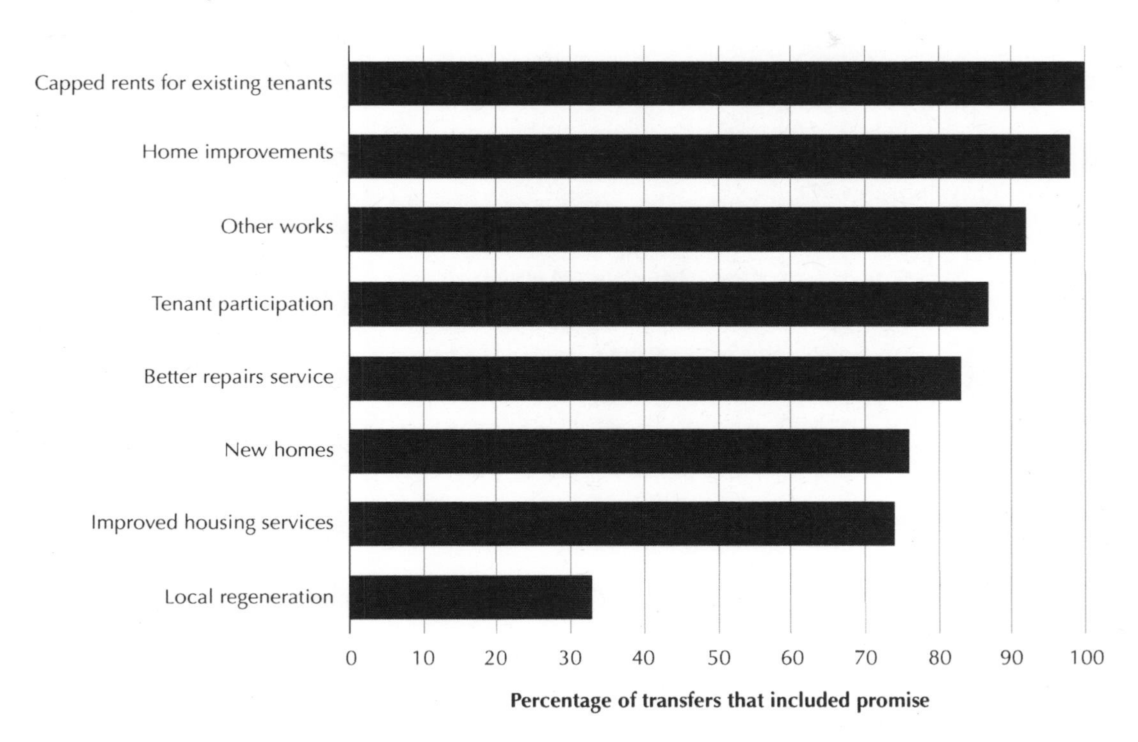

NOTE

Some RSLs regarded some items in consultation documents as "statements of intent" rather than promises. This explains why, for example, one transfer appeared to have omitted a promise about home improvements.

Source: National Audit Office survey of transfer RSLs (50 responses)

2.10 The promises made to tenants and the potential benefits of a change of landlord, including access to private finance, are key elements when tenants vote on whether a transfer should proceed. The promises also influence the transfer price - or in the case of ERCF transfers, the amount of grant required from the Office to make the transfer viable - and determine the financial demands arising on the RSL if the transfer goes ahead; the more generous the promises, the greater the likely financial cost of meeting them.

2.11 In our 10 case studies, some promises were stated in general terms, commonly aiming to provide the same services and at the same level that the local authorities had been providing before transfer or to complete "catch up" repairs within a certain time period. Other promises offered additional improvements that tenants could expect, such as upgraded kitchens and bathrooms. **Figure 8 overleaf** provides illustrative examples of well defined and poorly defined promises in our case studies. The well defined promises were clear about what improvements would be made to tenants' homes or about the number of new homes that would be built, and by when. Poorly defined promises were so vague as to be of little value in informing tenants about what they could expect to see in terms of home improvements or the building of new homes.

8 Examples of well defined and poorly defined promises

Some transfer promises were well defined, whilst others were poorly defined.

Well defined promises	Poorly defined promises
On improvements to homes:	
'Within three years the RSL plans to renew all windows and external doors, in double glazed UPVC, to all homes...; to install central heating to all properties either without it or where there are gas warm air systems, and to renew half the kitchens on the estate.' (Manchester City Council)	'The Association intends to prepare and implement a variety of annual modernisation programmes, including certain environmental works... and will seek to complete the Council's programme of bringing houses up to date.' (Thanet District Council)
On the development of new homes:	
'Approximately 500 additional homes will be provided over the first five years.' (Spelthorne Borough Council)	Some councils did not specify how many new homes would be built following the transfer.

Source: National Audit Office analysis of 10 case study transfers

9 Key benefits promised in the 10 case studies examined by the National Audit Office

There were substantial variations in the key benefits promised to tenants in our case studies.

Transfer RSL	Planned expenditure on catch up repairs and major works per home[2]	Guaranteed maximum annual rent increases over inflation (RPI +)	Promised development of new homes
Fortunegate Community Housing[1]	£25,323	0%	Rebuilding 579
Poplar HARCA[1]	£23,889	£2.25	112
Manchester & District HA	£6,530	3%	No promise
Broomleigh HA	£5,715	2%	No promise
Magna West Somerset HA	£3,910	1%	300
1066 HA	£3,160	2%	350[3]
Basingstoke & North Hampshire (Oakfern) HA	£3,063	1%	Number not specified
Thanet Community HA	£2,826	1%	93
Spelthorne HA	£2,672	1%	500
Hambleton (Broadacres) HA	£2,452	1%	60 per year

NOTES

1. Fortunegate Community Housing received an ERCF grant of £22.4 million to take on 1,481 homes (£15,125 per home) and Poplar HARCA received an ERCF grant of £35.2 million to take on 1,852 homes (£19,006 per home). These homes were much more rundown than the homes transferred in our other case studies.
2. The planned expenditure on repairs and major works per home is based on the first five years after transfer. The average local authority home in 1996 was in need of £2,240 of repair and replacement work over 10 years, suggesting that RSLs generally promise more renovation work on transfer properties.
3. Hastings Borough Council promised that the transfer could result in the development of up to 350 homes by 1066 Housing Association and other RSLs.

Source: National Audit Office analysis of files of the Office and 10 case study RSLs

2.12 The promised benefits in our 10 case studies varied significantly, as shown in **Figure 9.** Expenditure on catch up repairs and major works reflected the condition of the homes and their local environment. The variation in the guaranteed maximum rent increases reflected a combination of factors, such as the difference between transferring tenants' and new tenants' rent levels, RSLs' projected expenditure on repairs and improvements, development of new homes and running costs, including financing costs. Some RSLs promised to build more new homes than other RSLs, either from choice or where the stock was so poor as to warrant the demolition and rebuilding of properties. Examples of some of the benefits secured through three of our case study transfers are shown in **Figure 10 overleaf.**

2.13 The cost of more generous promises might be borne by local authorities through lower transfer receipts, by the Office through grants for ERCF transfers, by the RSLs themselves through lower surpluses or, as in the private housing sector more generally, by tenants through rents and charges for certain home improvements (as was general practice across the social housing sector). We found that RSLs had sought to recover some of the costs of the promises through a variety of means including higher rents for new tenants, high rent increases for existing tenants after the end of the rent guarantee period, and spreading some repairs and improvements work over long periods. Although new tenants may start at "target rent", which may be higher than existing tenants, the difference is now more controlled under the new rents regime taking effect from April 2002[10].

2.14 The Office and the Housing Corporation review all transfer prices, including the costs of the works programmes. The Office considers, however, that the scale and scope of promises are primarily for local authorities, RSLs and tenants to determine, reflecting local needs, expectations and circumstances.

Monitoring and evaluation of the outcome of individual transfers could have been more extensive

2.15 After transfer, the Housing Corporation maintains regular contact with all transfer RSLs as part of its routine regulation of the RSL sector as a whole. The Office has not, however, asked the Corporation to monitor and evaluate the performance against promises of individual transfers.

2.16 The Office has commissioned three reviews of the outcomes of a total of 14 different transfers (8 per cent of the total) under the LSVT and ERCF programmes:

- in 1995, researchers from the University of Birmingham's Centre for Urban and Regional Studies reported[11] on the outcomes of two transfers, with supporting evidence from another seven transfers. They found that promises were generally kept in both of the main case studies;
- in 1997, Pieda reported on the performance on nine transfer RSLs and found that there was no evidence that RSLs had failed to meet commitments to tenants to any significant degree; and
- in 2000, DTZ Pieda reported[12] that, based on tenant satisfaction levels in six RSLs, transfer had delivered benefits to tenants.

2.17 In 2001, the Office confirmed its intention to commission consultants to develop a system to monitor individual transfers and an evaluation framework to assess the overall impact of the LSVT programme. This project was commissioned in May 2002, and the Office expects to have the monitoring system and the evaluation framework in operation by Spring 2003.

2.18 For ERCF transfers, in 1997 the Office established arrangements for capturing baseline data, so that the impact of the transfers could be measured in subsequent years. The Office has not yet used the baselines to evaluate the performance of ERCF transfers because it considered that it was too soon to form a reliable view on the transfers' performance. However, it is now proposing to commission research during 2002-03 on learning the lessons from ERCF transfers, including following up the baseline data.

2.19 Since 1993, the Office has required local authorities to include in their transfer agreements with RSLs a deed of covenant, under which the RSLs agree to abide by the promises made to tenants. In the event of a breach of a covenant, the local authority is entitled to claim damages from the RSL, although to the Office's and Corporation's knowledge this has never happened. The Office does not, however, require local authorities in their ongoing strategic role to monitor RSLs' performance against promises after transfer. But, through councillors who are also members of RSLs' boards, authorities may be able to obtain feedback on the performance of RSLs. Only one of our 10 case studies, Manchester & District Housing Association,

10 *The rent reforms which came into effect in 2002 will ensure that by 2012 all social rents will be determined by the same formula related to properties' size, value and location regardless of whether the landlord is a local authority or an RSL. The Office requires all social landlords have plans setting out how they will meet the requirements of the reforms in place by April 2002.*

11 *Evaluating Large Scale Voluntary Transfers of Local Authority Housing (1995), Department of the Environment/David Mullins, Pat Niner, Moyra Riseborough.*

12 *Views on the Large Scale Voluntary Transfer Process (2000), Department of the Environment, Transport and the Regions/DTZ Pieda.*

10 Examples of benefits secured through transfers

Transfers can deliver significant benefits for tenants and other local residents.

Improvements carried out by Poplar Housing and Regeneration Community Association

Poplar HARCA received 1,852 homes from London Borough of Tower Hamlets in March 1998 with an ERCF grant of £35.2 million to support its ambitious programme for renovating the housing. By December 2001, Poplar HARCA had completed the refurbishment of these homes at a cost of £47 million. The transformation of the three estates was extensive, as illustrated in the before and after photos below:

Before

After

Regeneration activity carried out by Fortunegate Community Housing

While much of Fortunegate Community Housing's activity has focused on rebuilding or improving its 1,481 transferred homes, it has also made a significant contribution to local area regeneration. In particular:

- it has refurbished two community centres, equipped with computer suites for resident training and meeting areas.
- it also plans to build a third community centre; its Local Labour Initiatives Officer, funded through the Office's Single Regeneration Budget, helps local residents gain employment in the construction industry; and
- there have been substantial environmental works, including landscaping, improved lighting, better car parking, and safe play areas.

Broadacres Housing Association's development programme

Broadacres Housing Association (formerly Hambleton Housing Association)'s financial strength since its transfer in 1993 has allowed it to increase its stock through development and acquisition. Supported by grants from Hambleton District Council, the RSL had by August 2002 built an additional 467 homes and acquired 276 homes. The development work also improved the local environment by using land that had previously been contaminated.

Source: National Audit Office

reported annually to the transferring local authority on the delivery of promises, although Spelthorne Housing Association and Fortunegate Community Housing had provided their local authorities with a report on the delivery of promises since transfer, and Poplar HARCA provides its local authority with detailed performance information.

RSLs are generally delivering the expected benefits to tenants

2.20 Transfer RSLs have generally performed well in delivering the expected benefits to tenants, including the promises made during the consultation periods. RSLs have generally delivered the improvements to homes and services promised while restraining rent increases, but performed less well on local area regeneration and development of new homes. Figure 10 on page 20 provides examples of benefits secured through transfer for some of our case study RSLs. **Figure 11 overleaf** summarises our assessment of performance in each of the main benefit areas, based on the Office's research and our research from 10 case studies, including interviews with tenants, and our survey of 50 transfer RSLs. DTZ Pieda's 1997 report to the Office noted that 47 per cent of tenants considered that all promises had been met or exceeded, and only 9 per cent considered that the RSLs had failed to deliver.

2.21 We spoke to tenants at all 10 of our case study RSLs and obtained the latest tenant satisfaction surveys from the 50 RSLs in our survey. We found that most tenants considered that they had benefited from the transfer. Some of the comments made to us are shown below.

I'm very pleased with my new kitchen. It's worth the extra rent I have to pay...And the workmen who fitted it were polite and very obliging."

"I've had new windows put in. They're wonderful and I wasn't even expecting that from the transfer."

"I was promised new windows in two years, but I've not got them yet. These windows get wet, they make the house cold...and burglars could lift them out. And the housing association hasn't improved the repairs service - if anything they've got worse."

"My rent isn't very much - it's good value for money."

"The housing association has improved this area because it tackles anti-social behaviour."

Transfers are contributing towards the achievement of the government's Decent Homes standard.

2.22 In 2001 the Office introduced a new Public Services Agreement target to make all social housing decent by 2010. In November 2001 the Office surveyed 105 RSLs receiving transferred stock between April 1995 and March 2001, to examine progress towards its original expectation that most transfers would take five years to complete their improvement programmes. Transfer RSLs would not have planned their renovation programmes or collected data in relation to the new Decent Home standard prior to 2001. The survey found that 30 per cent of the 82 RSLs responding were making sufficient progress to suggest that all of their homes would meet the standard within five years of transfer (and 51 per cent of all the transferred homes would be "decent"), and that most RSLs would reach the standard 10 years after transfer. The data also suggests that up to 17 per cent of transferred homes might not meet the Decent Homes standard within 10 years of transfer, at current rates of progress. However, transfer RSLs are more optimistic about future progress, expecting on average to eradicate non-decent stock within around seven years of transfer **(Figure 12 on page 23).** The Office and Housing Corporation will be working with local authorities and all transfer RSLs to ensure that they have suitable plans for meeting the Decent Home target over time. Delivery against the Decent Home standard is now included in the Office's transfer guidelines, is reported on by RSLs, and will be included in the Office's planned monitoring and evaluation of the transfer programme.

Most transfers have resulted in RSLs with sound finances able to deliver the promised benefits to tenants

2.23 During the development of a transfer, the Office and the Housing Corporation seek to ensure that a local authority's homes are transferred to an RSL which is financially robust and capable of delivering the benefits promised. After transfer, the Corporation regulates the performance of the transfer RSLs including making assessments of whether they have adequate financial resources to meet their current, and future, business and financial commitments. Where it identifies a cause for concern about an RSL's performance, the Corporation may intervene to help resolve the problems.

Most RSLs with transferred stock are financially secure, although some have experienced financial difficulties

2.24 Relatively few transfer RSLs have experienced financial difficulty and most have stable finances and have expanded their operations since transfer. In their 1997

11 RSLs' performance against transfer promise

Transfer RSLs have generally performed well against the promises made to tenants

Area of promise	Office's research[1]	National Audit Office's research[2]	Our rating
Home improvements and other works	• 81% tenant satisfaction with the condition of homes (78% before transfer) • 81% tenant satisfaction with works undertaken (87% before transfer)	• RSLs said they had either met their promises on home improvements or were on schedule • On average, RSLs have improved 72% of their homes	4 houses
Rent increases	• 77% tenant satisfaction that rents are value for money (77% before transfer)	• RSLs visited had kept increases within guarantees • 83% of RSLs we surveyed said they had kept their rent increases within guideline figures	5 houses
Repairs and other housing services (for example, warden services)	• 63% tenant satisfaction with the quality of the repairs service (68 % before transfer) • 85% of tenants considered that housing services were at least as good as before transfer	• RSLs surveyed said they had met, exceeded or were on schedule to meet their promises on repairs • All RSLs we visited had met promises on housing services • RSLs are carrying out almost all repairs on time	4 houses
Tenant participation	No evidence	• RSLs had met their promises on tenant participation (mainly on membership of governing board) • Some RSLs provide financial support for tenants groups • Based on data submitted by RSLs to the Housing Corporation, 65% of tenants were satisfied with participation opportunities (by comparison, 49% of local authority tenants were satisfied - from the Office's Survey of English Housing 1999-2000)	4 houses
Regeneration	No evidence	• All transfers contribute to local area regeneration, but promises have not been a major feature of LSVTs • All but one of the RSLs we surveyed said that they had met their regeneration promises, or were on schedule	4 houses
Development of new homes	• Promises may become inappropriate where costs have increased or local circumstances changed	• 15% of RSLs surveyed said they had not met or were delayed in meeting development pomises	3 houses

Key:
1 house = poor performance
to
5 houses = excellent performance

NOTES

1. The Office's research is based on the DTZ Pieda report (2000) and its Surveys of English Housing.
2. The National Audit Office's research comprises visits to 10 RSLs, a survey of 50 RSLs and analysis of Housing Corporation information.

Source: National Audit Office

12 The Office's April 2001 assessment of the progress being made by 82 RSLs in bringing transferred stock up to the Decent Homes standard

Based on survey responses from RSLs, the Office predicted that around 80 per cent of the RSLs' stock will have been made decent 10 years after transfer

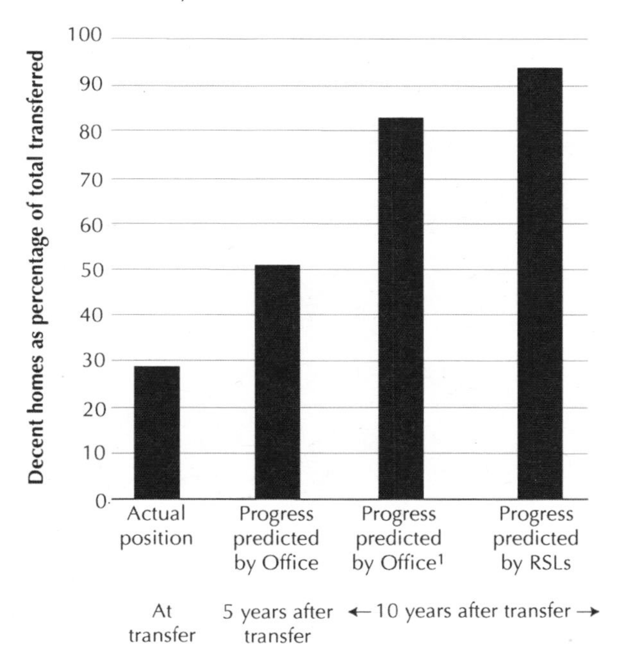

NOTES

1. Progress predicted by the Office is based on rates of progress reported as at April 2001.

Source: National Audit Office, using data from the Office of the Deputy Prime Minister

report for the Office, Pieda concluded that the original income and expenditure forecasts of 9 RSLs set up under the LSVT programme had proved to be highly inaccurate in the five years after transfer. Some RSLs were performing better than expected and some worse than expected **(Figure 13 overleaf)**. All of the RSLs examined by Pieda had met or exceeded their rent income projections, and 5 of the 9 RSLs were generating larger surpluses than expected in their original business plans. The 4 RSLs with lower than expected surpluses had all spent more on development than originally planned, and had brought forward their development programmes owing to out-performance of their business plans. Across the 9 RSLs, surpluses over five years exceeded forecasts by a net total of £8 million. Surpluses before development costs exceeded forecasts by a net total of £45 million.

2.25 The Housing Corporation, together with the National Housing Federation, carried out an analysis of the RSL sector's financial performance and financial strength in 2001[13], including transfer RSLs. The analysis showed that RSLs were generally in a sound financial position although there appeared to be a growing number who were facing some financial difficulties. Transfer RSLs' business plans are commonly based on high and increasing debt levels in the early years after transfer, reflecting the outflows in the early years to purchase and renovate the homes, and hence transfer RSLs generally appeared to be less strong than traditional RSLs. The Corporation's key measure for transfer RSLs was how well they were performing compared to their business plans, and on this basis, the financial strength of transfer RSLs was generally good. Under its new regulatory regime, the Corporation is due to complete its assessment of the financial strength of each RSL holding more than 50 dwellings by the end of March 2003.

2.26 The RSLs in our 10 case studies considered that their financial strength was in part due to favourable economic circumstances. The low interest rates in recent years have allowed them to manage within the tighter rent regimes introduced by government. The majority of the RSLs also benefited from their transferred homes being in relatively good condition and located in more prosperous parts of the country where demand is more certain.

2.27 The Housing Corporation's data on the regulatory history of RSLs found that 29 transfer RSLs (19 per cent) had at some point since transfer given rise to serious concerns at the Corporation in respect of their financial viability or governance. Of these, five were still subject to the Corporation's intervention at the end of November 2002. The Corporation intervened in the management of four transfer RSLs within one year of the transfer taking place, owing to potential fraud in two cases and financial difficulties in the other two cases.

13 *2001 Global Accounts and Sector Analysis of Housing Associations, The Housing Corporation and the National Housing Federation.*

13 Key results of the Pieda review of the performance of 9 RSLs set up under the LSVT programme compared with the RSLs' original business plans, 1996

A 1997 review by Pieda of 9 RSLs set up under the LSVT programme found that some RSLs were performing better than expected and some worse than expected.

Income, cost or surplus	Number of cases where performance was:	
	better than expected	worse than expected
Rental income	7	0
Management costs	4	5
Maintenance costs	3	6
Major repairs and improvements costs	4	5
Development costs	4	2
Overall surpluses	5	4

Source: "Evaluation of the performance of Large Scale Voluntary Transfer Housing Associations", Pieda plc (1997)

2.28 The Corporation had intervened in two of the RSLs included in our 10 case studies. In the case of 1066 Housing Association, its financial viability, and hence its ability to deliver a good service to tenants, were at risk and it was obliged to seek a merger with a stronger RSL (see box below). The Housing Corporation considers that the principal lesson from this case has been the importance of robust stock condition information at the time of transfer. By contrast, Broomleigh Housing Association's difficulties, which related to management weaknesses in the development of new homes, did not impair its financial strength or ability to deliver promises. The Corporation's intervention lasted around eight months, by which time it was satisfied that the RSL's improvements to its internal procedures were effective.

Intervention by the Housing Corporation in an RSL after transfer

- 1066 Housing Association was vulnerable to financial difficulties from the time of transfer in February 1996. It had not made sufficient allowance for work needed to improve some of its less desirable stock, or for any problems of rent losses through low demand. The inflexibility of its funding model did not allow it to respond easily to unforeseen adverse circumstances.
- Four years after transfer, the RSL experienced uncertainty about the cost of future repairs and improvements together with a high rate of voids at one of its estates. The RSL tried to refinance its debts and extend the term of the original loan it took out upon transfer. However, the lenders would not agree the new business plan. At around the same time, the Housing Corporation intervened and made two statutory appointments to the RSL's board. The RSL's board then removed its Chief Executive and appointed a temporary special manager. And the RSL decided to seek a merger with another RSL.
- The impact of rent reforms remained a problem because the RSL would not be allowed to make annual rent increases of the size that it had previously planned to make. In 2002, the RSL merged with Amicus Group, another RSL that had been set up to receive transferred stock. Amicus Group estimated that the problems had resulted in one-off costs of around £1.2 million, but that efficiency savings secured through the merger would soon recoup these costs.

Part 3

The financial effects of transfer

The Office and local authorities use a model to inform negotiations over the transfer price

3.1 Transfer prices have to be negotiated between the local authority and the receiving RSL, with the advice of consultants. To provide a baseline for these negotiations, local authorities use a model agreed with HM Treasury, known as the Tenanted Market Value (TMV) model, to estimate the value of the homes to be transferred. Originally developed by local authorities, the Office has adopted and refined the model for use in all transfers. The TMV is usually substantially less than the open market value because the valuation reflects, as is appropriate, the intended continued use of the properties for social housing rather than the most profitable alternative use.

3.2 The TMV model provides a baseline to inform the local authority's negotiation of the transfer price. These negotiations, however, must also take into account:

- Lenders' preparedness to finance the deal. The RSL's lenders will make their own assessment of the value, and may increase their interest rate to reflect higher risk or may not be prepared to provide finance if the transfer price is, in their estimation, too high.
- Tenant involvement in the transfer process. The transfer valuation is based on a set of promises to tenants about rents, improvements to homes and better amenities. As the transfer terms are developed, the local authority and the RSL may revise these promises in the light of tenants' views.

3.3 As a result of these factors, the transfer price may differ from the Tenanted Market Value, as shown in the following examples:

- In one of our ERCF case studies, Fortunegate Community Housing, to help achieve funding for the transaction, the Office relaxed its rules on valuation and agreed that the RSL would receive additional grant to fund improvements to homes, costing up to £6.6 million, which would normally be charged to the tenants and existing leaseholders. The Office later increased the grant by a further £6 million to secure the private finance. The Office considered these increases to be appropriate because of existing high rent levels and to secure leaseholder involvement in a major redevelopment.
- The lender backing the transfer to Thanet Community Housing Association declined to finance the transfer at the £25.7 million value indicated by the TMV model. The Office consented to the transfer at a price of £21.5 million, representing a reduction of 16 per cent, on the grounds that the lender would not otherwise fund the transfer and a companion transfer in Thanet had resulted in a "no" vote by tenants.
- The Office increased its ERCF grant to Poplar HARCA by £11.7 million (50 per cent) to make the transfer viable and fundable.

We found no evidence in these cases, however, that the Office had asked whether other lenders would have been prepared to fund the transfer at or nearer to the original valuation.

Transfer terms are intended to be cost-neutral for the receiving RSL, but this may not be achievable

3.4 The TMV is calculated as the net present value of the RSL's projected stream of income from renting out the transferred stock, less its expenditure flows. In theory, therefore, a transfer price based on this transfer value should leave the RSL no better or worse off. In practice, however, cost neutrality for the RSL is unlikely to be achieved for a number of reasons, set out in the rest of this section.

The model uses a fixed time period whereas property lives may vary

3.5 The TMV model nets off an RSL's projected income and expenditure flows over 30 years. The model does not provide for the homes and the land on which they sit to have any residual value after year 30, reflecting the increasing uncertainties of the income, including demand for the homes, and expenditure such as major works, further into the future. In some transfers, homes may be in considerable disrepair or difficult to let, in which case they may not have an economic life of 30 years.

3.6 Property life can have a major impact on the transfer value. Using the data for our 8 LSVT case studies, we estimated that if the life of properties had been assessed as 40 years the potential transfer value would have increased by £51 million (14 per cent) compared with the total actual transfer prices of £356 million **(Figure 14)**. If a 40 year life were assumed across all transfers to date, then the total transfer receipts might have increased by around £700 million. These illustrative figures do, however, assume that finance would still have been available, and that surpluses would remain constant whereas they might diminish if a further major renewal programme was required after 30 years. The RSLs in our case studies, however, considered that their transferred stock would have a value 30 years after transfer, in part because of the better repairs and maintenance associated with transfers. They were also expecting higher surpluses after year 30 even after allowing for the cost of renewals programmes. The analysis suggests therefore that there is a need for a more flexible approach to determining the lifetime of transferred housing, tailored more to the circumstances of the stock proposed for transfer.

The discount rate used in the model has been higher than RSLs' cost of capital

3.7 The TMV model applies a discount rate to bring an RSL's future income and expenditure into present value terms. In accordance with HM Treasury's *Green Book*, the Office intends that the discount rate reflects the RSLs' cost of capital.

3.8 At the outset of the LSVT programme in December 1988, the Office agreed with HM Treasury that local authorities should use a discount rate of 8 per cent in calculating their TMV transfer values. This rate was used on all transfers until 1999, reflecting the financial risk of the new RSLs and the additional margins that the landlords would have to pay in their private finance deals with lenders. By 1999, the LSVT and ERCF transfer programmes had built up a significant track record, reducing the risk to lenders. Also, by then landlords could borrow at much lower interest rates than before, and some local authorities expressed concern to the Office that their housing was being sold too cheaply using an 8 per cent rate. The Office, in consultation with HM Treasury, therefore reduced the discount rate to 7 per cent for transfers in the 1999-2000 transfer programme, reserving the option of allowing some local authorities to use a discount rate of 8 per cent in view of lenders' concerns that some urban transfers might not be financially viable at a lower rate.

3.9 The Office has allowed local authorities on the 2000-01, 2001-02 and 2002-03 transfer programmes to choose a discount rate of 6, 7 or 8 per cent. By July 2002, there had been 20 transfers using a 7 per cent discount rate, one at 6.5 per cent and one at 6 per cent. The Office considers that 6 per cent might be

14 Case study transfer values calculated over different time periods

In the 8 case studies examined by the National Audit Office, transfer values would have been higher had the TMV model used a life longer than 30 years, and assuming finance would still have been available.

TMV period (years)	Combined transfer value (£ million)	Increase over 30-year transfer price (£ million)	(per cent)
30	356	Not applicable	Not applicable
40	407	51	14
50	431	75	21

NOTE

The computation assumes that the RSLs' annual surpluses would remain constant beyond year 30 whereas they may diminish if a further major renewal programme was required in the period.

Source: National Audit Office

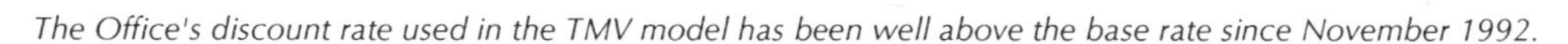

15 Comparison of discount rates used in the valuation model with interest rates in real terms, 1989 to 2002

The Office's discount rate used in the TMV model has been well above the base rate since November 1992.

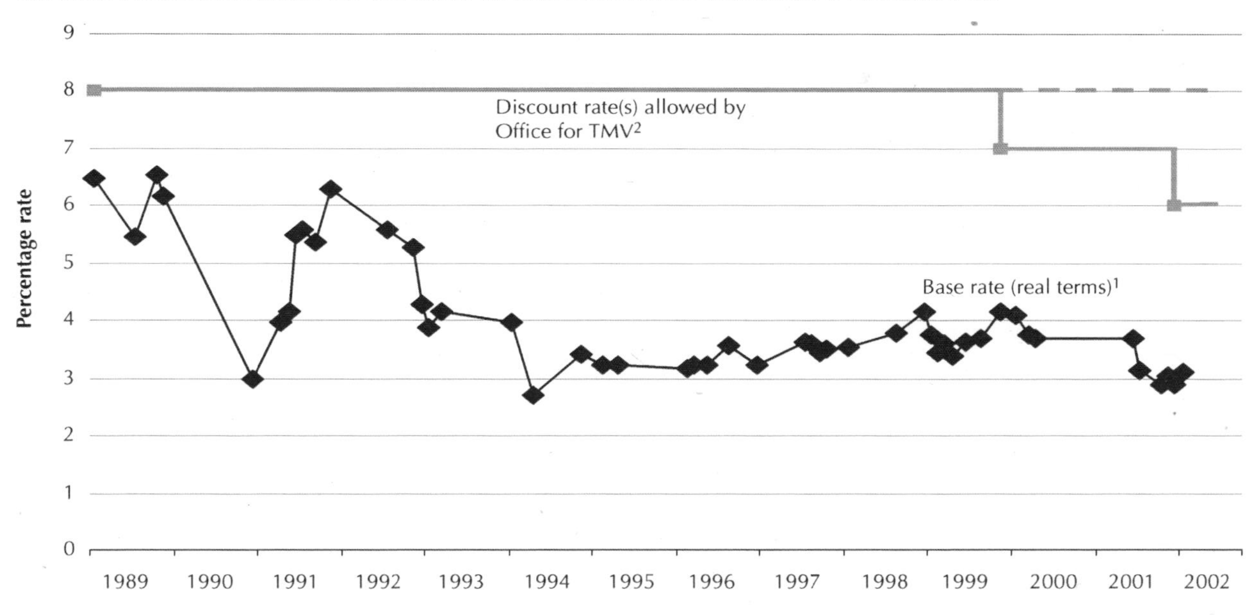

NOTES

1. Base rate (real terms) is the base rate in money terms less the current annual rate of change in the Retail Prices Index at the time.
2. The Office's discount rate is stated in real terms. Since 1999, the Office has allowed local authorities to use a range of discount rates.

Source: National Audit Office, using data published by the Bank of England and the Office for National Statistics.

appropriate where the stock is in relatively good condition and/or demand for the homes is buoyant. It does not allow any local authority to use a lower rate than this, even if a transfer would be viable at a lower rate or if the RSL is likely to secure funding from lenders at a lower rate, to prevent local authorities looking to maximise their receipt unreasonably.

3.10 The discount rate in the model has therefore been much higher than the actual cost of capital for much of the LSVT programme's life:

- Interest base rates fell during 1992 and have since remained much lower than in the early years of the programme. **Figure 15** shows that in real terms the base interest rate has stayed at around 4 per cent or less since November 1992.
- Loan margins above base rates, to reflect lenders' views on risk, were between 1.25 per cent and 1.5 per cent for early transfer RSLs. By 1997, margins were very low, as little as 0.5 per cent, and transfer RSLs in the 2000-01 programme secured loans with margins ranging from 0.1 per cent to 0.5 per cent above base rates. These margins exclude arrangement and other fees received by lenders, which are borne by local authorities (rather than the RSL).

3.11 The discount rate can have a significant financial impact on the calculated transfer value. The 1995 transfer to Basingstoke & North Hampshire Housing Association (now Oakfern Housing Association), one of our case studies, was undertaken at an actual transfer price of £51.9 million, calculated using the Office's 8 per cent discount rate. At a discount rate of 4.5 per cent, the RSL's real interest rate on its loans arranged at the time of transfer, the calculated value would have been £79.4 million (53 per cent higher). However, this higher transfer value could only have been achieved in practice if lenders were still prepared to fund the transfer, and the Office believes that there is no evidence that a higher price would have been achievable had one been sought.

A more flexible model would better meet the objective of cost neutrality

3.12 Cost neutrality is therefore unlikely to be achieved through the use of a fixed model to calculate the tenanted market value. As shown above, property lives and discount rates can alter significantly the Tenanted Market Value produced by the model, although the impact may be less in transfers of poorer urban housing which are expected to predominate in future. A closer approximation to cost neutrality might be achieved if the model were more flexible, for example by taking greater account of the quality of the housing to be transferred in deciding the time period over which cashflows should be discounted, and using a cost of capital likely to be closer to that of an RSL acquiring the stock. The transfer price reflects a price at which lenders are prepared to provide finance but a more flexible approach to estimate the transfer value would provide a range of values against which an RSL's offer and lender's willingness to support could be tested. The Tenanted Market Value is not always the achievable transfer price in practice, but it is a key element in starting negotiations, and in considering the value for money of the transfer proposal.

Some post-transfer events can also affect the RSL's financial position

3.13 Post transfer events can also have an impact on the cost neutral position. Some changes in the transfer RSL's financial position will reflect better or worse performance or changing circumstances that cannot reasonably be forecast at the time of transfer - a natural consequence of the risk transfer inherent in the programme. But other impacts may reflect events such as the refinancing of loans by RSLs after transfer, the sale of property under the Right To Buy scheme, or the sale or redevelopment of land after transfer. The possibility of these more foreseeable events occurring has not always been recognised in the transfer terms, as explained below. Where these events turn out in favour of an RSL, leading to a more favourable financial position than anticipated at transfer, these surpluses are available to the RSL for use in support of its wider purposes. The use of surpluses is discussed in paragraphs 3.19 to 3.22.

RSLs may refinance their loans after transfer

3.14 The interest rates charged by lenders on the loans that RSLs take out at the time of transfer reflect both the prevailing market rates and the lenders' assessments of the riskiness of an RSL's business. In May 2002 Ernst and Young found that the majority of financially strong RSLs receiving good quality stock refinanced their loan facilities within the first two to three years after transfer. In four of our 10 case studies, the RSLs had refinanced their original loans, all securing cheaper finance as a result, and another two were in the process of refinancing.

Right To Buy sales may generate additional receipts

3.15 Transfer tenants can buy their homes under the Right To Buy (RTB) scheme. Before transfer, it is difficult to predict how many tenants might subsequently exercise their right to purchase their homes and to take account of them in determining the transfer value. The Office therefore suggests that local authorities should agree to share the receipts from RTB sales with RSLs.

3.16 We found that three of the RSLs involved in our 10 case studies had benefited from Right To Buy sales without this being reflected in the transfer price.

- Eight days before transfer, West Somerset District Council advised the Office that it was unable to agree with Magna West Somerset Housing Association on the sharing of RTB receipts, which the authority considered would not be worth much. By March 2001, the RSL had received £3.6 million from RTB sales and it expected more receipts in future. Based on the terms of a typical sharing agreement amongst our 10 case studies, we estimated that the local authority may have forgone around £1.7 million (7 per cent of the transfer value).
- There was no sharing agreement in the transfer from Tower Hamlets Council to Poplar HARCA because the local authority was unwilling to commit to one. It was concerned that the low prices of homes in East London could result in it having to compensate the RSL for any shortfalls in rental income after transfer. By February 2002, the RSL had completed the sale of 80 homes and it expected to sell more homes at a reduced rate in the future. We estimated that the receipts foregone may have been around £0.9 million, equivalent to 3 per cent of the RSL's ERCF grant.
- Basingstoke & Deane Borough Council's sharing agreement with Oakfern Housing Association gave it a share of RTB receipts for only the first 428 houses and 61 flats sold out of a total of 4,175 homes eligible for RTB. The Office expressed concern to the council about the arrangement, but the agreement was not changed before transfer. The limit was reached in 1999, four years after transfer. Since then, the RSL has generated further RTB receipts of over £6 million. We estimate that the local authority may have foregone receipts of some £2.2 million (4 per cent of the transfer value).

Some RSLs have sold or redeveloped land and property after transfer

3.17 In two of our case studies (Broomleigh Housing Association and Oakfern Housing Association), the RSLs had demolished some of their worst homes and redeveloped the areas for social housing and private homes, and had also converted some former social housing into homes for market renting (albeit, in Oakfern's case, on a temporary basis). There were no arrangements for the RSLs to share with the local authority any surpluses that might accrue from such disposal or change of use, but in both these cases the RSLs consulted their local authorities and planned to use surpluses to further their social housing objectives.

3.18 In another case, the local authority transferred land and properties to the RSL (Poplar HARCA) for nil consideration. Four years after transfer, the RSL sold part of the land to private developers for £2 million, having demolished 114 properties on the land at a cost of £1.3 million, a net gain of £0.7 million. The transaction gave the RSL additional finance to improve the area by changing the mixture of types of homes, making the homes more lettable and improving future income streams. Neither the local authority nor the Office could share in the proceeds or the increased income from the disposal nor can they directly influence how such surpluses are used (although these must be in accordance with the not-for-profit objects of an RSL). The RSL also plans to make further disposals of land obtained as part of the original transfer.

The Office and the Housing Corporation have limited influence over how RSLs use any post-transfer gains

Transfer RSLs may use their surpluses in a variety of ways

3.19 RSLs are independent, not-for-profit organisations set up to meet the needs of their tenants and their local communities. RSLs do not distribute any dividends. When a new RSL registers with the Housing Corporation, the Corporation requires that its principal object must be to provide social rented housing, which must account for at least 50 per cent of the RSL's activity. Up to 49 per cent of activity may be on non-social housing activities. Although this can include, for example, market renting, it can also include housing for students, key workers and other groups which help to develop sustainable communities. RSLs must use their surpluses in accordance with their own articles of association and objects. While RSLs' boards can amend their articles and objects, they must obtain the Housing Corporation's approval.

3.20 The Corporation can intervene if RSLs use their surpluses for purposes other than those set out in their articles and objectives or if RSLs carry out more than 49 per cent of their activities in non-social housing areas. And the Corporation may seek to influence RSLs' use of their surpluses where RSLs apply for grant funding from the Corporation for new housing projects.

3.21 Respondents to our survey of transfer RSLs reported that, on average, 84 per cent of their turnover came from transferred homes and 94 per cent came from social housing activities. RSLs do also engage in non-social housing activities; for example, half of those responding to our survey were letting properties at market rents. However, the most diversified of the RSLs responding to our survey still derived 75 per cent of its turnover from social housing activities.

3.22 Pieda reported to the Office in 1997 that one of the most important issues for the transfer programmes was the need for the Office to institute controls over the use of surpluses generated by RSLs after transfer. The Office considered that so long as RSLs used their surpluses within their articles of association and objects, their activities would further the government's housing objectives, be they to provide and improve social housing or to improve the choice, availability and quality of homes in the market rented sector. Cost neutrality at the time of transfer is difficult to achieve in practice due to the parameters set in the Office's model, and uncertainties inherent in forecasts and, in our view, the Housing Corporation should look to increase their influence over how any surpluses from the transfer process are deployed by RSLs to ensure they support overall government aims to improve social housing provision and develop sustainable communities.

Competition may improve transfer terms but complicate choice

3.23 One of the aims of the transfer programme is to provide tenants with a choice of landlord. The Office has not, however, until recently expected local authorities to use competition, or offer tenants a choice of RSL, because of difficulties associated with how best to fit competition into the transfer process without reducing the involvement of tenants or putting at risk tenants' support for transfer. In around two-thirds of transfers, local authorities have sold their homes to new organisations created from authorities' housing departments specifically to receive the stock. Local authorities transferred stock to existing RSLs in the other 50 transfers. However, all but 5 of the 50 transfers have been partial stock transfers involving an insufficient number of homes to enable a new, financially viable RSL to be set up. There has therefore been little competition in the transfer programmes to date.

Some local authorities have less incentive to achieve a higher transfer price

3.24 Until 1999, some local authorities were unable to transfer their homes because the capital receipts would not be enough to repay all of their housing debt. Since 1999, however, the Office has agreed to repay such overhanging debt. Authorities likely to have overhanging debt know that the capital receipt would have to be used to repay debt and associated redemption penalties. If the actual transfer price is lower than originally expected, then the Office repays more of the debt and may, since February 2003, pay the redemption penalties. An authority will only benefit financially if the transfer price is greater than the value of the overhanging debt.

3.25 The Office reviewed those four authorities on the 2001 transfer programme that had held competitions. They noted the risk that overhanging debt authorities could have less incentive to maximise receipts, particularly if this was at the expense of offering better services to tenants. By July 2002, there had been seven transfers involving overhanging debt totalling £515 million. All but one of the local authorities would have required at least double the transfer price to have generated a receipt in excess of the overhanging debt, supporting the potential risk identified that there is less incentive to maximise the transfer value in such cases. The Office expects that a significant proportion of future transfers[14] will involve overhanging debt because authorities in this position were unable to transfer all of their stock earlier in the transfer programmes.

The Office has taken steps to bring more competition and choice into the transfer process, with some success

3.26 In its April 2000 Housing Green Paper, Quality and Choice: A Decent Home for All, the government considered it unhealthy to identify a single RSL as the only route to transfer. RSLs should bid against each other to acquire and manage local authority stock, both on the price to be paid for homes and the services to be provided after transfer. The December 2000 Housing Policy Statement, *Quality and Choice: A Decent Home for All*, stated that local authorities would be required to provide evidence that tenants had been given a choice of landlord, including existing and new RSLs, to receive the transferring stock.

3.27 In 2001, the Office encouraged greater choice but did not make competition a requirement for gaining a place on the transfer programme or for obtaining final consent to transfer. It now expects all authorities on the 2002 transfer programme (i.e. those transferring between April 2002 and March 2004) and beyond to show how they have complied with the Office's policy on landlord choice.

3.28 In January 2002, the Office completed a review of the experience of four local authorities on the 2001-02 transfer programme which had selected their RSLs through formal competition. It concluded that the pilots had shown that competition could deliver a better final product, but that there was no clear evidence that competition had generated substantially increased sales receipts. We note, however, that two of the four authorities increased their transfer values by £8 million (although this proposed transfer was later withdrawn for reasons unconnected with price) and £0.4 million respectively. In the two other transfers, the selected RSLs agreed to pay all or half of the local authorities' set up costs.

14 In 1999, the Office estimated that total housing debt attributed to the 3.3m local authority dwellings in England was approximately £20 billion, with average debt per dwelling of £6,000. The scale of potential overhanging debt was more difficult to determine as it depended on the stock valuation and amount of housing debt in each authority at the moment of transfer.

The cost and value for money of the programmes

3.29 The Office has not carried out any evaluations of the actual costs and benefits of the LSVT and ERCF transfer programmes, although it has commissioned research to set up a framework that will enable it to evaluate future transfers under the LSVT programme. The Office believes that the good progress of ERCF transfers, means that it is now appropriate to commission the evaluation of individual transfers and the programme. It is now commissioning an evaluation that will use baseline data collected at the time of the transfers. The Office has also compared the costs and benefits of hypothetical transfer programmes with the costs and benefits of alternative options to transfer. The Office had used these assessments to inform subsequent policy making, and particularly whether to continue with the LSVT programme.

The Office's original assessment of the cost of the LSVT programme looked at the impact on public expenditure aggregates

3.30 The Office, with HM Treasury, carried out a first assessment of the LSVT programme in 1993. There had, by then, been 23 transfers involving 118,000 homes. The Office modelled the financial effects of a hypothetical transfer programme consisting of 100 transfers and involving 500,000 homes over the period 1994-95 to 1998-99. It estimated that over 30 years a transfer programme would reduce the Public Sector Borrowing Requirement (PSBR) by £240 million (£301 million at 2002 prices), or £480 per home (£601 at 2002 prices), compared with local authorities retaining their stock and continuing with their existing level of funding for capital maintenance. On this basis, the Office decided that the LSVT programme should continue.

3.31 As agreed with the Treasury, the Office looked at the PSBR impact of each transfer and the programme as a whole. The Office could, however, in our view also have looked at the actual cost to the taxpayer. The actual cost excludes transactions which occur solely within the public sector, such as central government subsidy of local authority housing, and transactions which are not a direct consequence of transfer, such as the local authorities' use of capital receipts to improve local services.

The Office's more recent assessments have considered financial costs to the taxpayer and the non-quantifiable benefits arising from the programme

3.32 In 1999, the Office carried out a new assessment of the costs of the future LSVT programme, calculating the financial cost to the taxpayer of transfer and comparing it with that of leaving the stock in the local authority sector and continuing with their existing level of funding for capital maintenance (which would achieve more modest renovation more slowly). The Office estimated that transferring all 3.4 million of the remaining local authority housing would cost the taxpayer £13 billion (£3,800 per home) over 30 years, while transferring 1.4 million homes (broadly equivalent to continuing the then rate of transfer) would cost £5.5 billion (£4,000 per home) over the same period. These were hypothetical scenarios with the Office recognising that transfer was one option available to local authorities when they came to assess ways of improving the condition and management of their housing.

3.33 Until 1998, most local authorities had only two options for managing their housing stock - retention or transfer - although the Office did not allow authorities to undertake additional borrowing equivalent to the levels of private finance available for transfers. However, local authorities now have more alternatives to stock transfer: using the Private Finance Initiative; managing their stock through an Arm's Length Management Company[15]; or, since April 2001, using the new Major Repairs Allowance to renovate retained stock.

3.34 In 2000, the Office compared the financial costs and benefits of transfer with those of retention and renovation by local authorities with similar access to funding as an RSL. The Office estimated that an illustrative 5-year LSVT programme transferring, say, 1 million homes would cost the taxpayer between £2.4 billion and £3 billion (£2,400 and £3,000 per home) over 30 years. Transfer would cost between £100 million and £700 million more over 30 years than the alternative of fully funded local authority retention and renovation, because:

- rents were expected to rise more rapidly after transfer to an RSL, resulting in higher Housing Benefit costs[16];
- RSLs' borrowing costs were higher than those of local authorities; and
- there were significant transaction costs involved in setting up a transfer.

15 *Arm's Length Management Companies (ALMOs) were introduced in April 2001. An ALMO is owned by a local authority and is responsible for managing the authority's housing stock, separating the authority's management role from its strategic role. Where they can demonstrate high standards, ALMOs receive additional funding from the Office.*

16 *The rent reforms which came into effect in 2002 will ensure that by 2012 all social rents will be determined by the same formula related to properties' size, value and location regardless of whether the landlord is a local authority or an RSL. The Office requires all social landlords have plans setting out how they will meet the requirements of the reforms.*

3.36 In 2001, the Office revised its assessment of the financial effects of transfer compared with those for retention and renovation by local authorities. Based on a hypothetical 5-year LSVT programme involving 1 million homes it estimated the cost to the taxpayer to be £4.2 billion (£4,200 per home) spread over a 30 year period, which was £1.3 billion (£1,300 per home) more than fully funded local authority retention and renovation. This increase in forecast costs was mainly due to the introduction of a new rent regime for local authorities and RSLs in April 2002, which had the effect of holding down RSL rents to bring about a convergence of RSL and local authority rents over the next 10 years.

3.37 The 1999, 2000 and 2001 assessments suggested that transfers were more expensive than retention in financial cost terms but the Office considers that the unquantifiable benefits arising from transfer, such as the transfer of risk, the accelerated achievement of improvements, the greater tenant participation and community regeneration provided by RSLs, offset the additional monetary cost. Risks transferred include income (for example, rent levels) and cost risks (for example, maintenance and financing costs), and the risks arising from shortfalls in demand. The Office also considers the additional financial cost to be small in the context of over £15 billion allocated to housing expenditure in the 5-year period 2001-02 to 2005-06. As our report shows, the programme has been largely successful in delivering improvements in services to tenants and in transferring the financial risks in holding properties for letting.

3.38 The Office's 2001 calculations reflected the application of a standard Treasury discount rate of 6 per cent to the option of local authority retention. New HM Treasury guidance now suggests that departments should apply a lower discount rate, 3.5 per cent, to their policy appraisals. Using this rate would increase the additional cost of the same transfer programme across a 30 year period over the cost of local authority retention and renovation, because the long term financial benefits of retention become more valuable with a lower discount rate. However, the Office is considering the implications of the new guidance on its appraisal of the transfer programme, and in particular the adjustments which might be needed to the cost/benefit calculations to reflect the transfer of risk to RSLs and the tendency for over-optimism in the appraisal of the outcome of projects. These adjustments might offset the increase in the cost differential between transfer and retention arising from the application of the lower discount rate.

Appendix 1 What happens when a transfer occurs

1 There are a number of transactions between the four key stakeholders affected by transfers.

- **Local authorities** transfer some or all of their social housing assets and liabilities to a Registered Social Landlord, together with some of their staff. Authorities receive in return a capital receipt from the RSL. Local authorities use these receipts to cover the cost of administering the transfer and to repay any central government housing loans. Local authorities must pay a levy to the Office if any proceeds remain. The remainder of the receipt is available for the local authority to spend. Where capital receipts from transfers are less than local authorities' housing loans, the Office pays off authorities' overhanging debt and any early redemption penalties. Under the ERCF programme, where transferred homes had a negative value, the central government paid grants to the local authority.

A Transactions between the four key stakeholders affected by transfers

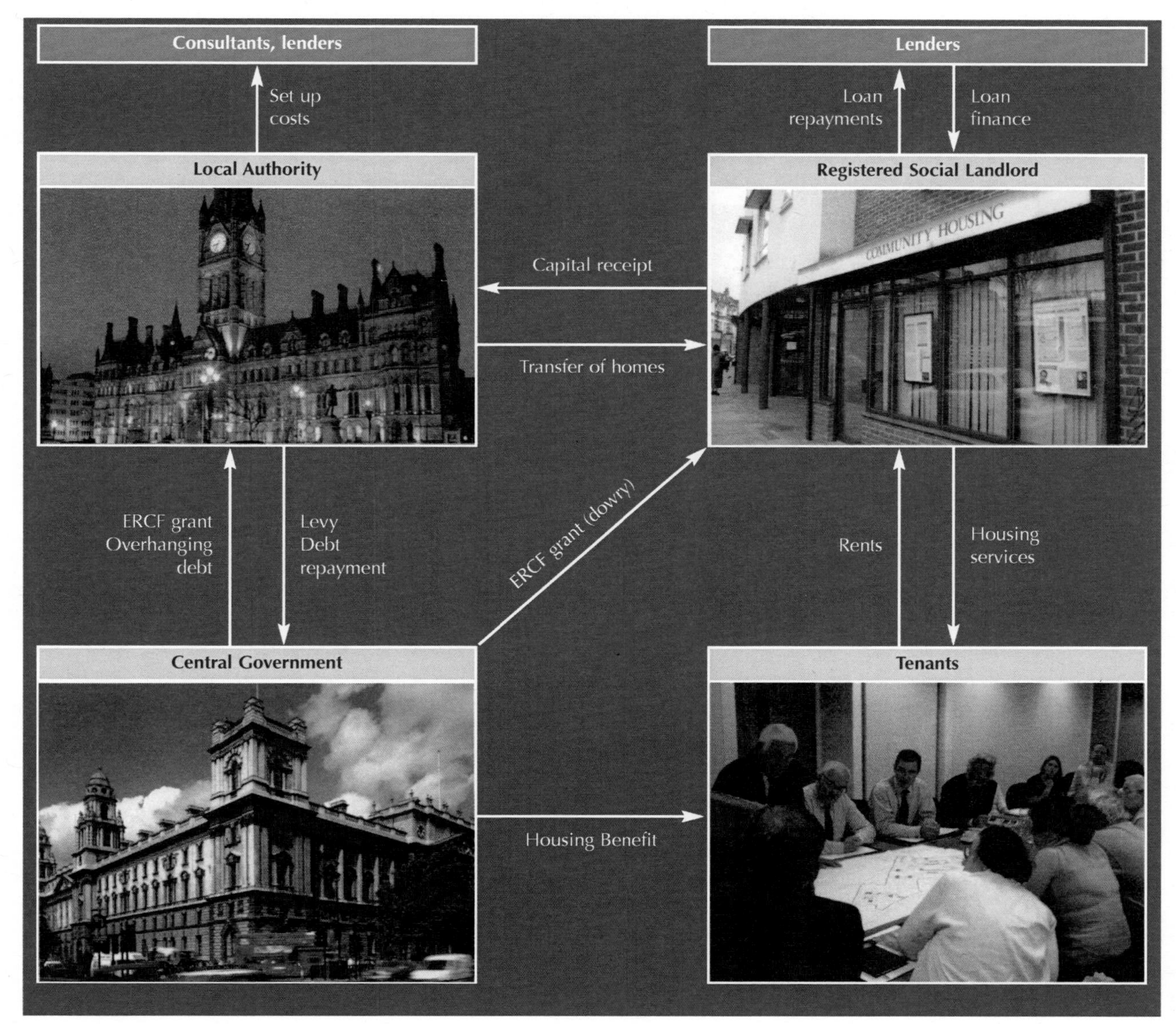

Source: National Audit Office

- **RSLs** borrow from commercial lenders to buy, repair and improve authorities' homes. RSLs provide housing services to tenants in the transferred properties, in return for rent and service charges. Under the ERCF programme grants are made by central government to RSLs as a dowry for taking on properties with a negative value.
- **Tenants** transfer to the new landlord together with the housing and they benefit from the repairs, improvements and better housing services of the RSL. Tenants, in return, pay rent and service charges to the RSL. Most tenants pay rent from Housing Benefit.
- **Central Government** receives part of the local authorities' capital receipts as repayment of housing loans, and a levy on any remaining receipts. Central government pays off any local authority housing debt that is not covered by the receipts. Central government's Housing Benefit payments increase after transfer where rents rise to reflect RSLs' investment in housing or any change arising from rent reform. Under the ERCF programme, Central government also paid grants to local authorities and RSLs.

The transactions and flows are set out in **Figure A on page 33**.

2 **Figure B** below shows the main financial effects of a transfer. The Office intends that the transfer price (or Tenanted Market Value) paid by the RSL to the local authority is equivalent to the RSL's expected future surpluses, which are likely to be similar to the authority's foregone financial surpluses. If this is the case in practice, the main costs to the taxpayer arise from any increases in Housing Benefit costs that result from the higher RSL rents[17], the costs of any renovations that cannot be recouped in higher rents, any grants paid to the RSL to support the transfer and the costs of setting up the transfer. The wider effects of transfer on public borrowing include transactions between central and local government and changes in local authority capital spending. These elements are not a cost of transfer to the taxpayer.

3 All transfers cost money to set up, including consultants' fees, the costs of arranging RSLs' loans, and the costs of administering transfers at the Office, the Housing Corporation and local authorities. The Office's data show that local authorities' transaction costs have averaged £1.7 million per transfer (£430 per home). The main components are the cost of arranging loans, consultancy and legal fees.

B The financial effects of a transfer

The transfer of council housing has a cost to the taxpayer and an impact on public sector borrowing, which takes account of wider effects.

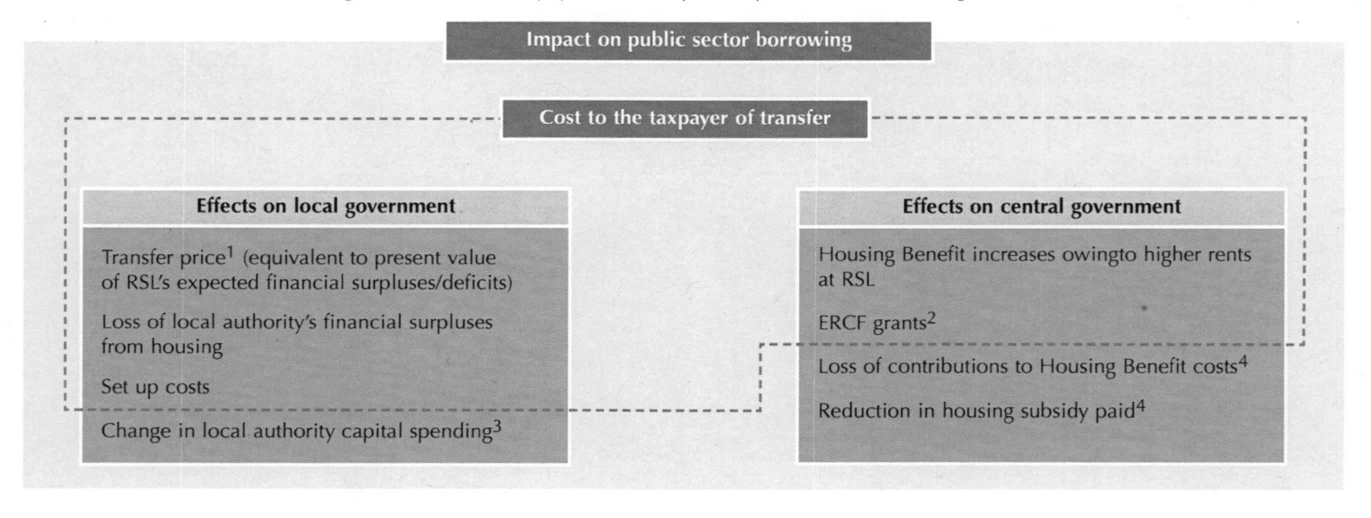

NOTE

1. This model excludes any additional rent costs to tenants not in receipt of full Housing Benefit, which has no impact on the taxpayer.
2. Each transfer has a transfer price, paid by the RSL to the local authority, or an ERCF grant, paid by the Office to the RSL. The transfer price is a financial benefit to the taxpayer to be set against other costs.
3. The change in local authority capital spending is assumed not to represent a net cost of transfer because it should result in assets of equivalent value.
4. The two effects on central government that are not part of the cost to the taxpayer are transactions between central and local government.

Source: National Audit Office

17 *The rent reforms which came into effect in 2002 will ensure that by 2012 all social rents will be determined by the same formula related to properties' size, value and location regardless of whether the landlord is a local authority or an RSL.*

Appendix 2 Study methodology

Case studies

We obtained much of our evidence from visits to 10 RSLs that received transferred housing between April 1992 and March 1998. These case studies enabled us to observe and quantify the local outcomes of the national transfer programme in detail. Although the sample of RSLs was not statistically representative, we were able to use this evidence to illustrate trends identified in a larger survey of RSLs (see below). A short description of each of the case study RSLs is in Appendix 3.

Before the visits, we discussed the performance of each case study RSL with regulatory staff at the Housing Corporation and we examined the Office's documentary records of the transfers. For the two oldest of our case study transfers, the files had been destroyed so we were unable to obtain some pre-transfer information for these cases.

During each visit, we interviewed management and other staff and tenants, viewed the condition of the housing stock and examined relevant documents including statutory accounts, business plans and management board minutes. The Audit Commission accompanied us on these visits, and they also visited the transferring local authorities. We are very grateful to the RSLs we visited for their co-operation and assistance.

Survey of transfer RSLs

We conducted a postal survey of 60 RSLs that received transferred stock between April 1992 and March 1998. Using this period ensured that the RSLs had had time to deliver. The response rate was 83 per cent. To validate responses we requested supporting documentation from all respondents and we visited 4 RSLs. The survey covered: the delivery of promises to tenants; improvement works and stock condition; rents and service charges; tenant participation; and finance and diversification.

The full survey results can be found on our web site at www.nao.gov.uk/publications/nao_reports/0203/0203496_survey.pdf

Interviews

We conducted a number of interviews with officers of the Office of the Deputy Prime Minister and the Housing Corporation. We also conducted semi-structured interviews with representatives of organisations that are involved in or affected by the transfer programmes:

- Amicus (formerly the AEEU)
- The Chartered Institute of Housing
- The Council of Mortgage Lenders
- Defend Council Housing
- HACAS Chapman Hendy
- The Local Government Association
- Nationwide Building Society
- HM Treasury
- Unison

We also sought internal, expert advice on some of the technical aspects of transfer from an NAO economist and an expert on Public Private Partnerships.

Review of other reports and evaluations

We reviewed other reports and evaluations, some of which have been published, including:

- *Evaluating Large Scale Voluntary Transfers of Local Authority Housing: An Interim Report,* Department of the Environment / David Mullins, Pat Niner, Moyra Riseborough, 1992
- *Evaluating Large Scale Voluntary Transfers of Local Authority Housing,* Department of the Environment / David Mullins, Pat Niner, Moyra Riseborough, 1995

- *Evaluation of the Performance of Large Voluntary Transfer Housing Associations,* Pieda plc, 1997
- *Housing Associations: A Viable Financial Future,* HACAS Consulting / The Chartered Institute of Housing, 1999
- *Views on the Large Scale Voluntary Transfer Process,* Department of the Environment, Transport and the Regions / DTZ Pieda, 2000
- *Survey of the delivery of Decent Homes by transfer RSLs,* Department of Transport, Local Government and the Regions, 2002
- *Sources of Finance for Stock Transfers,* Office of the Deputy Prime Minister / Ernst & Young, 2002
- *Beyond Bricks and Mortar: Bringing Regeneration into Stock Transfer,* HACAS Chapman Hendy / The Chartered Institute of Housing, 2002

Performance Indicators

The Housing Corporation collects data over a range of performance indicators for the entire RSL sector on an annual basis, and we used this evidence to examine the performance of transfer RSLs. We also used Housing Corporation data on the condition of RSL housing stock.

Expert panel

We set up an expert panel to provide advice on our study approach and findings. The members of the panel were:

Stephen Duckworth
Projects Director, National Housing Federation

Steve Fox
Stock Transfer Registration Unit, Housing Corporation

Gill Green
Senior Manager, Audit Commission

Simon Llewellyn
Branch Head, Housing Associations and Private Finance 4, Office of the Deputy Prime Minister

David Mullins
Reader in Housing Studies, Centre for Urban and Regional Studies, University of Birmingham

Sarah Webb
Divisional Manager, Community Housing Task Force, Office of the Deputy Prime Minister

Appendix 3 Transfer case studies examined by the National Audit Office

Case study 1: Broomleigh Housing Association (part of The Affinity Homes Group)

Transfer details

Transfer date:	6 April 1992
Transferring authority:	London Borough of Bromley
Number of homes:	12,393
Transfer price:	£117.6 million
Private loans:	£136 million
Transfer ballot result:	55% in favour

The RSL was set up by the Council to take over the transferred stock that comprised brick built flats and terraced houses in good condition.

Broomleigh HA has spent £131 million on repairs and improvements (£10,600 per home) and built or acquired about 1,000 new homes since transfer.

67% of tenants are satisfied with the landlord.

Broomleigh HA was placed in Housing Corporation supervision between March and December 1999, until weaknesses in the control of new development were resolved.

Transfer promises

- Rent increases limited to inflation plus 2% for 4 years
- General improvements to homes and environment
- No development promise
- 5/15 Board members to be tenants

Improved housing

Case study 2: Broadacres Housing Association (formerly known as Hambleton Housing Association)

Transfer details

Transfer date:	29 April 1993
Transferring authority:	Hambleton District Council (North Yorkshire)
Number of homes:	4,268
Transfer price:	£33.5 million
Private loans:	£55 million
Transfer ballot result:	78% in favour

The RSL was set up by the Council to take over its homes, which were mainly traditionally built houses in good condition.

Broadacres HA has spent £12.7 million on repairs and improvements (£3,000 per home) and built or acquired 743 new homes since transfer.

97% of tenants are satisfied with their landlord.

The Housing Corporation has assessed Broadacres HA's performance as satisfactory under its regulatory regime.

Transfer promises

- Rent increases limited to inflation plus 1% for 2 years and plus 2% for the next 2 years
- Internal improvements
- At least 60 new homes per year
- 6/18 Board members to be tenants

Redeveloped housing

Case study 3: Thanet Community Housing Association

Transfer details

Transfer date:	19 December 1994
Transferring authority:	Thanet District Council (Kent)
Number of homes:	2,658 (split transfer)
Transfer price:	£21.5 million
Private loans:	£34 million
Transfer ballot result:	51% in favour

The RSL was set up by the Council to take over its special needs housing for older people and people with disabilities although the transfer also included some general needs housing. The properties were mainly brick built houses with some flats, generally all in good condition. The proposed simultaneous transfer of the rest of the Council's housing failed at the ballot.

Thanet Community HA has spent £19.5 million on repairs and improvements (£7,300 per home) and built or acquired about 125 new homes since transfer.

88% of tenants are satisfied with their landlord.

The Housing Corporation has assessed the RSL's performance as satisfactory under its regulatory regime.

Transfer promises

- Rent increases limited to inflation plus 1% for 3 years
- General improvements
- 250 new homes (between two separate RSLs)
- 5/15 Board members to be tenants

Transferred sheltered housing

Case study 4: Oakfern Housing Association (part of the Sentinel Housing Group and formerly known as Basingstoke & North Hampshire Housing Association)

Transfer details

Transfer date:	20 March 1995
Transferring authority:	Basingstoke and Deane Borough Council
Number of homes:	4,432 (split transfer)
Transfer price:	£51.9 million
Private loans:	£85 million
Transfer ballot result:	52% in favour

The RSL was set up by the Council to take over its homes that were a mixture of brick built houses, modern flats and pre-reinforced concrete houses (PRCs). The brick houses were in good condition but the flats and PRCs required significant remedial work.

Oakfern HA has spent £38 million on repairs and improvements (£8,500 per home) and built or acquired approximately 350 new homes since transfer.

77% of tenants are satisfied with their landlord.

The Housing Corporation has assessed Oakfern HA's performance as satisfactory under its regulatory regime.

Transfer promises

- Rent increases limited to inflation plus 1% for 5 years
- Internal and environmental improvements
- No new homes promised
- 4/15 Board members to be tenants

New development adjoining freehold property

Case study 5: Spelthorne Housing Association (now part of the Apex Housing Group)

Transfer details

Transfer date:	19 January 1996
Transferring authority:	Spelthorne Borough Council (Surrey)
Number of homes:	3,465
Transfer price:	£50.1 million
Private loans:	£90 million
Transfer ballot result:	73% in favour

The RSL was set up to take over the Council's housing stock, a mixture of houses, maisonettes and flats, including some sheltered units.

Spelthorne HA has spent £13.9 million on repairs and improvements (£4,000 per home) and built or acquired 476 new homes since transfer. 99% of homes now meet the Decent Homes standard.

87% of tenants are satisfied with their landlord.

The Housing Corporation has assessed Spelthorne's performance as satisfactory under its regulatory regime.

Transfer promises

- Rent increases limited to inflation plus 1% for 5 years
- Internal improvements
- 500 homes in five years
- 6/18 Board members to be tenants

Improved housing

Case study 6: Ten Sixty-Six Housing Association (now part of the Amicus Group)

Transfer details

Transfer date:	21 February 1996
Transferring authority:	Hastings Borough Council
Number of homes:	4,560
Transfer price:	£45.8 million
Private loans:	£88 million
Transfer ballot result:	69% in favour

The RSL was set up by the Council to take over its housing, comprising houses, flats and maisonettes in fair condition.

1066 HA has spent £19.8 million on repairs and improvements (£4,300 per home) and built or acquired 68 new homes since transfer.

The RSL has not yet estimated how many of its homes meet the Decent Homes standard, but it reports that there are no significant repairs backlogs.

80% of tenants are satisfied with their landlord.

The Housing Corporation placed 1066 HA into supervision in July 2000 due to the association's financial difficulties. This led to 1066 HA's merger in 2002 with the Amicus Group, another transfer RSL.

Transfer promises

- Rent increases limited to inflation plus 2% for 5 years
- General improvements
- Up to 350 homes
- 6/18 Board members to be tenants

Transferred housing estate

Case study 7: Manchester & District Housing Association (now part of the Harvest Housing Group)

Transfer details

Transfer date:	29 March 1996
Transferring authority:	Manchester City Council
Number of homes:	1,409 (partial transfer)
Transfer price:	£10.1 million
Private loans:	£25 million
Transfer ballot result:	90% in favour

Manchester & District Housing Association was an existing RSL that took over the Council's Partington housing estate which comprised of mainly brick-built houses and a small number of flats and maisonettes in considerable disrepair.

The RSL has spent £18.6 million on repairs and improvements (£13,200 per home) and not built or acquired any homes on the Partington estate. It expected all its transferred homes to meet the Decent Homes standard by the end of 2002.

86% of tenants are satisfied with their landlord (includes all RSL tenants, not just at Partington).

The Housing Corporation has assessed the RSL's performance as satisfactory under its regulatory regime.

Transfer promises

- Rent increases limited to inflation plus 3% for 9 years
- Internal and environmental improvements
- No new homes promised
- 4/12 committee members to be tenants with possibility of up to 8 tenants

Before environmental improvements

Case study 8: Poplar Housing and Regeneration Community Association (Poplar HARCA)

Transfer details

Transfer date:	23 March 1998
Transferring authority:	London Borough of Tower Hamlets
Number of homes:	1,852 (partial transfer)
Transfer price:	£35.2 million grant
Private loans:	£53 million
Transfer ballot result:	72% in favour

The RSL was set up by the Council to take over some of its more rundown estates, comprising of mainly flats and maisonettes.

Poplar HARCA has spent £46.6 million on repairs and improvements (£25,200 per home) and built or acquired 47 new homes since transfer. 100% of homes now meet the Decent Homes standard.

There have been two further transfers of housing from the Council to this RSL.

57% of tenants are satisfied with their landlord.

The Housing Corporation has assessed Poplar HARCA's performance as satisfactory under its regulatory regime.

Transfer promises

- Rent increases limited to inflation + £2.25 for 7 years
- Internal, external and environmental works
- 112 homes
- Community facilities
- 6/18 Board members to be tenants

After major renovation

Case study 9: Fortunegate Community Housing (part of Ealing Family Housing Group)

Transfer details

Transfer date:	30 March 1998
Transferring authority:	London Borough of Brent
Number of homes:	1,481 (partial transfer)
Transfer price:	£22.4 million grant (plus £2.4 million grant for set up costs)
Private loans:	£49 million
Transfer ballot result:	75% in favour

Fortunegate Community Housing is a specially created subsidiary of an existing RSL. The transferred housing is a mixture of brick-built flats and houses and 1970s pre-fabricated flats in generally poor condition.

Fortunegate has spent £38 million on repairs, improvements and redevelopment (£30,000 per refurbished home and £74,000 per rebuilt home), including the demolition of 216 properties. 38% of homes now meet the Decent Homes standard.

53% of tenants are satisfied with their landlord (65% excluding tenants whose homes are still to be demolished).

The Housing Corporation has assessed Fortunegate's performance as satisfactory.

Transfer promises

- Rent increases limited to inflation for 5 years
- Internal, external and environmental works
- 579 redeveloped homes
- 4 community facilities, jobs for residents
- 6/18 Board members to be tenants

Before major renovation

Case study 10: Magna West Somerset Housing Association (part of the Magna Housing Group)

Transfer details

Transfer date:	30 March 1998
Transferring authority:	West Somerset District Council
Number of homes:	1,869
Transfer price:	£25.7 million
Private loans:	£55 million
Transfer ballot result:	62% in favour

Magna West Somerset HA, a new subsidiary of an existing RSL (Magna Housing Association), took over the Council's housing which was a mixture of brick built houses and flats, in generally good condition, and pre-reinforced concrete houses which needed to be re-built.

The RSL has spent £14 million on repairs and improvements (£7,500 per home) and built or acquired 47 new homes since transfer. It expects to have cleared its backlog of repairs and improvements by mid-2003.

77% of tenants are satisfied with their landlord.

The Housing Corporation has assessed Magna West Somerset HA's performance as satisfactory under its regulatory regime. But it placed the RSL's parent under supervision from October 1998 to August 2000 for governance problems.

Transfer promises

- Rent increases limited to inflation plus 1% for 6 years
- Internal and external improvements
- 300 homes
- 5/15 Board members to be tenants

Before renovation

Appendix 4 Summary of the Audit Commission report *Housing After Transfer*

The Audit Commission's report, published in November 2002, focuses on how local authorities carry out their responsibilities after the transfer of their housing stock and what this means for people who depend on local authorities for housing services. In carrying out its research, the Commission used information from housing inspections, visited the areas studied by the National Audit Office and other local authorities and RSLs, and conducted surveys of councillors and local authorities. The main findings are set out below.

Transfer is not just about changing landlords

When a local authority sells most or all of its homes, this is not just a matter for existing tenants and staff providing a landlord service; it affects all local people because of changes to authority finances, the way the authority works and all its retained housing services. Transfer always brings more local investment in the short term because RSLs are able to borrow money to buy and improve the council housing stock. The level of investment and the amount of capital received by the local authority transfer often provides authorities with a net capital receipt after repayment of debt, which is not directly linked to current housing authority need or performance. It is left to local authorities to decide how or if they wish to spend or invest these net receipts; they do not have to spend them on housing or related services.

There have been important changes to the transfer programme over time

Changes to government policy objectives have affected the outcomes of transfers. Early transfers were typically smaller districts with high value homes. Since 2000, whole stock transfer has become a viable option for a wider range of authorities, including those with higher levels of social need, that would not obtain a capital receipt from transfer.

The impact of transfer on the strategic focus of local authorities has varied

Some authorities have taken the opportunity of transfer to refocus on different housing issues across tenures, aligning housing with other services to address local priorities. But transfer does not automatically widen thinking or mean that staff can deliver more. Some authorities have lost interest in housing, maintaining only a minimal presence to fulfil statutory requirements. Improvements to the strategic role require the authorities' planning, commitment and resources.

Retained front line housing services are affected

Stock transfer changes the way in which many local authority frontline services are delivered; they do not always improve. There are new risks as well as opportunities for authorities after transfer so they need to work differently. In particular, local authorities must concentrate on the coordination of services after transfer, including housing benefit and information, advice and homelessness services.

Clarity about local governance and partnerships is important

Systems of local governance after transfer are more complex for local authorities, and clarity is needed to prevent gaps in services or duplication of effort. Partners should look at the role of authority-appointed RSL board members, lead members, officers and outside agencies in monitoring, accountability, liaison and advocacy for housing issues. Maintaining and improving cross-agency partnerships is critical. Clarity on leadership and responsibility is also important for work that cuts across traditional services but is often linked to housing, such as work to reduce anti-social behaviour or to regenerate areas.

Changes before and after transfer are needed to maximise local effectiveness

Problems after transfer could be minimised if there were changes to the way that transfers are planned by local authorities. Work is also needed after transfer to maintain local leadership, deliver effective housing strategies, focus on the needs and views of service users and manage relationships with housing providers to improve local services and quality of life.

The Commission's report is available from its website, http://www.audit-commission.gov.uk.